Operational Excellence Handbook
A Must Have for Those Embarking On a Journey of Transformation and Continuous Improvement

Operational Excellence Handbook

A Must Have for Those Embarking On a Journey of Transformation and Continuous Improvement

Rod Baxter

VALUE GENERATION PARTNERS

2015

Copyright © 2015 by Rod Baxter

All rights reserved. This book or any portion thereof may not be reproduced or used in any manner whatsoever without the express written permission of the publisher, except for the use of brief quotations in a book review or scholarly journal.

First Edition: 2015

ISBN 978-1-329-18432-9

Value Generation Partners, LLC
8083 San Vista Circle
Naples, Florida 34109
info@valuegenerationpartners.com

www.valuegenerationpartners.com

Contents

Acknowledgements ix
Preface xi
Introduction: Operational Excellence 1

Section 1: Strategic Approach 3
  McKinsey 7S Framework 3
  Strategy Maps 6
    Prioritizing and Correlating Projects to Strategies 9
  Balanced and Cascading Scorecards 12
  Quality Management System 14

Section 2: Cultural Leadership 19
  Change Leadership 19
  Conflict Resolution 24
  Consensus Building 27
  Motivating Individuals 29
  Team Building 33

Section 3: Practices and Methodologies 39
  Facilitating Continuous Improvement Events 39
    Improving Cross-Functional Processes 42
    Finding and Eliminating Waste 46
    Reducing Cost of Quality 48
  A3 PDCA, LSS DMAIC, and DfLSS DMADV 51
    A3 Thinking 54
    Lean Six Sigma (LSS) DMAIC 56
    Design for Lean Six Sigma (DfLSS) DMADV 59
  Theory of Constraints (TOC) 62

Section 4: Project Management 65
  Project Lifecycle Management 66
    Project Toolbox 68
      Business Case Proposal 72
      Charter 75
      Requirements Document 77
      Financial Reporting 80
      Stakeholder Management Plan 83

Contents

Work Breakdown Structure (WBS) 87
Resource Plan 90
Contact List 93
Schedule and Gantt Chart 94
Communication Plan 98
    Informative Communication 101
    Concise Communications 102
Quality Management Plan 103
Procurement Management Plan 106
Risk Management Plan 108
Issue Management Plan 111
Change Control Plan 113
Lessons-Learned Plan 115
Checklist 117
Close-out and Sign-off 120

Section 5: Tool Selection and Use 123
5 Why 124
Action Plan 126
Affinity Diagram 128
Agenda and Minutes 130
Brainstorming 132
Cause-and-Effect (C&E) Diagram 134
Cause-and-Effect (X-Y) Matrix 136
Control Plan 138
Data Collection Plan 141
Decision Tree 146
Fault Tree Analysis (FTA) 148
Force Field Analysis 152
Failure Modes and Effects Analysis (FMEA) 154
Goals - SMART 158
House of Quality (Quality Function Deployment) .. 160
Impact/Effort Analysis 165
Kano Model Analysis 168
Mind Mapping 171
Multivoting 174
Nominal Group Technique (NGT) 176
Pairwise Comparison 177
Process Maps 180
Pugh Matrix 185
RACI 188
Seven Basic Quality Tools 191

Contents

SIPOC 194
Six Thinking Hats 197
Solution-Selection Matrix 200
Status Report 202
SWOT Analysis 204
Training Plan 207

Summary 211

Index 213

Acknowledgements

I would like to recognize my colleagues and coworkers, and thank my various coaches and mentors, from the many countries, companies, and cultures I have had the opportunity to work with, for, and learn from during the past thirty-five years. They have added such richness to my life and career, and I've learned so very much from their knowledge, skills, and perspectives. These experiences and relationships, along with the many challenging and rewarding assignments I've had the opportunity to learn and grow from, have provided me the knowledge, experience, and expertise to present the content that made this book possible.

I would especially like to acknowledge and thank my wife Kelli, who is my thirty-three year partner in life, and in our consulting firm Value Generation Partners. It was Kelli who suggested we write a book that may provide value for business leaders and make a difference in their organizations.

Kelli has spent countless hours brainstorming with me, and reading and rereading the many drafted versions of this book. Her extensive experience in leadership consulting, continuous improvement, and project management has provided her with the necessary tools to serve as editor of this technical work. Kelli has challenged and checked facts, improved the content and flow, corrected grammar, and added significantly to the subject matter. Her input and support made this book a rich resource for those who choose to add it to their library.

Preface

This Operational Excellence Handbook contains 70 chapters organized in five sections describing strategy, culture, methodologies, project management, and tools that are helpful to create immediate and sustainable value for your organization.

To achieve a communications- and team-based culture of continuous improvement, this handbook is appropriate for organizations' leaders and practitioners alike. As you travel on your value generation journey, you will wish to select the appropriate approach, methodologies, and tools – based on your organization's current situation, future strategies and goals, resource availability and limitations, as well as urgency and schedule needs – that will provide immediate value.

This handbook is the culmination of thirty-five years of experience in the practical application of project management, quality management, continuous improvement, transformation, and operational excellence. It is intended to provide you with information to help you determine the appropriate approach, process, methodology, and tools that are right for you and your organization, and how to apply them based on your specific needs.

It's important to note that not all organizations are on the same value generation journey. Likely the starting point and the destination differ by organization. One organization's journey may be focused on full-scale transformation; another organization's continuous improvement efforts may be specific to cost reduction and quality improvement.

Many of the tools and approaches described in this handbook may be used alone or together as an overall approach to your value generation journey. The speed and magnitude of results will vary based on the organization's complexity and commitment to change. Regardless of your value generation journey's path, appropriate attention to commitment, discipline, and rigor must be given to the five key elements of operational excellence.

Strategic Approach + Cultural Leadership + Methodology + Project Management + Tools = Operational Excellence

With the purchase of this book, you are eligible to receive a complementary MS Excel® file, which contains the templates referenced in these chapters.

To download your copy of the Operational Excellence Toolbox, enter into your web browser the URL below.

http://www.valuegenerationpartners.com/downloads.html

Then, please complete and submit the download form. Thank you.

Introduction: Operational Excellence

While it is very important to clearly define operational excellence, it is bigger than a single definition. We must not simply define operational excellence; we must communicate, discuss, measure, live and breathe it, in order to achieve its benefits and sustain the culture.

Let us examine the term *operational excellence* and its components. *Operational* refers to the activities and functions of your business; *excellence* refers to brilliance and superiority. Is there brilliance in the activities and superiority in the functions of your organization? If so, how do you measure and, subsequently, achieve operational excellence? Vince Lombardi said, "Perfection is not attainable. But if we chase perfection, we can catch excellence."

Will Durant, in The Story of Philosophy, summed up Aristotle's writings as, "We are what we repeatedly do. Excellence, then, is not an act, but a habit." Successfully achieving operational excellence is the culmination of bringing together the following key elements, all of which must be approached with consistent and repeated commitment, passion, rigor, and discipline.

- **Strategy** – leadership creates vision and values for the organization; these are distilled into strategic focus and direction
- **Metrics** – scorecards balanced to strategies, and cascading through entire organization
- **Culture** – all individuals understand the strategy, and are authorized for, accountable for, and owners of achieving the strategic vision through continuous improvement of processes, products, and services
- **Systems** – organization implements holistic, integrated quality

Introduction: Operational Excellence

management system and processes
- **Methodology** – applying rigor and discipline of Design for Lean Six Sigma, Lean Six Sigma, A3 Thinking, or Theory of Constraints
- **Project Management** – applying rigor and discipline of Project Management Institute's (PMI®'s) Project Management Body of Knowledge (PMBOK®)
- **Tools** – solution delivery (processes, products, and services), problem solving, and continuous improvement

Employing these critical elements listed above – along with a foundation of well-communicated and understood purpose, vision, mission, and set of values – creates operational excellence. Supporting operational excellence is a culture of continuous improvement that utilizes the rigor of project management. Other supportive elements of an operational excellence culture are strategy, metrics, systems, and methodologies.

Benefits of operational excellence include:

- Improved revenue and profit
- Improved customer satisfaction
- Collaborative team environment
- Improved processes, products, and services
- Improved compliance and risk prevention
- Improved organizational effectiveness
- Improved employee engagement
- Sustained, intentional organizational culture

The ensuing sections and chapters provide ingredients necessary to define, develop, and execute an operational excellence transformation. We wish you much success in your pursuit of operational excellence, thereby generating greater organizational value!

Section 1: Strategic Approach

One key element of the operational excellence transformation is strategic approach. This section of the handbook includes chapters related specifically to proven operational excellence strategic approaches.

- McKinsey 7S Framework
- Strategy Maps
    - Prioritizing and Correlating Projects to Strategies
- Balanced and Cascading Scorecards
- Quality Management System

Please consider these as essential ingredients to successful strategic approaches supporting the value generation journey.

McKinsey 7S Framework

One model that is effective for evaluating and gaging your organization's ability to perform and adapt to transformational change is the McKinsey 7S Framework. It may be employed to analyze and understand the current organization, define a future-state organization, determine gaps between the current and future state, define an action plan to transform the organization, and close gaps. The McKinsey 7S Framework first appeared in a *Business Horizons* article, in June 1980, by Tom Peters, Bob Waterman, and Julien Phillips; it was titled, "Structure Is Not Organization."

The McKinsey 7S Framework consists of seven interdependent elements that must be fully aligned in order for an organization to perform effectively today, and to move forward in the future, with transformational change. By applying the model to your organization, it becomes evident as to which of the seven elements must be reinforced to ensure – or realigned to improve – performance. Independent of your transformational change effort, the model sup-

Section 1: Strategic Approach

ports thorough understanding of the relationship of the elements and the need to take a holistic approach.

McKinsey 7S Framework consists of four "soft" and three "hard" elements as listed below:

Soft Elements

1. **Shared Values** – includes organization's culture, vision, and core values
2. **Style** – how the organization's leadership behaves and works together
3. **Staff** – includes individuals' attitudes, behaviors, motivation; how they are trained, on boarded, promoted, evaluated, etc.
4. **Skills** - capabilities and proficiencies of the organization and its associates

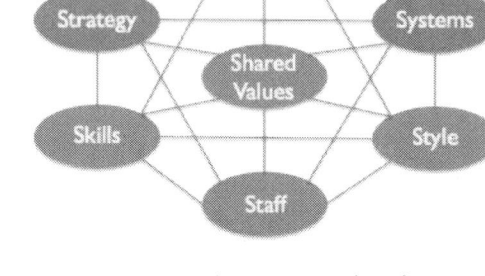

Hard Elements

5. **Strategy** – organization's plans and actions to respond to its stakeholders, customers, and competitors
6. **Structure** – how the organization operates, ranging from centralized, decentralized, hierarchical, or matrix approach
7. **Systems** – formal and informal processes used by individuals to complete activities and tasks

McKinsey 7S Framework may be applied when:

- New or changing strategies are being considered
- There is a desire to improve organizational performance
- Organization is conducting transformation or change initiatives
- Organization wishes to understand the effects of change initiatives
- Organization is generating non-organic growth through acquisitions

Section 1: Strategic Approach

Benefits of the McKinsey 7S Framework include:

- Provide a collaborative team environment
- Provide an approach to improve and ensure performance
- Increase focus and attention on change and transformation initiatives
- Provide an approach for effectively implementing change
- Provide a consistent approach for analyzing, aligning, and reinforcing elements of change

McKinsey 7S Framework Process:

This process may be used to eliminate gaps and misalignments in the current state or to define a future state without gaps and misalignments.

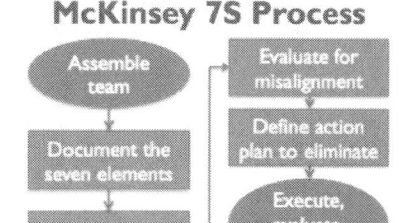

1. Assemble a cross-functional team of participants who are briefed and come prepared to engage in the process
2. Define and document the seven elements of the organization
    a. Soft elements: Shared Values, Style, Staff, Skills
    b. Hard elements: Strategy, Structure, Systems
3. Evaluate the seven elements to identify and document gaps using the "McKinsey 7S Gap Log"

McKinsey 7S Process

Assemble team → Evaluate for misalignment → Define action plan to eliminate → Execute, evaluate, and adjust ← Evaluate for gaps ← Document the seven elements

VALUE GENERATION PARTNERS — McKinsey 7S Gap Log

Project Name:	
Project Manager:	Date:

Element	Gap
Shared Values	
Style	
Staff	
Skills	
Strategy	
Structure	
System	

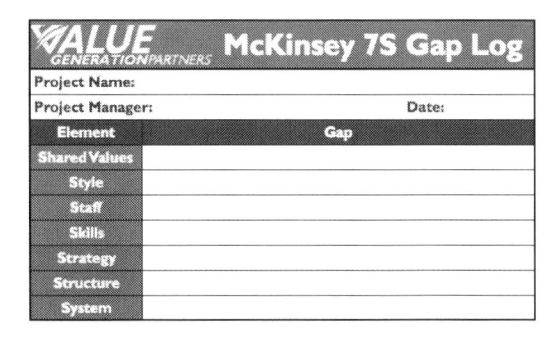

4. Evaluate the seven elements to identify and document misalignments using the McKinsey 7S Misalignment Matrix

Section 1: Strategic Approach

	Shared Values	Style	Staff	Skills	Strategy	Structure	System
Shared Values							
Style							
Staff							
Skills							
Strategy							
Structure							
System							

McKinsey 7S Misalignment Matrix (Project Name, Project Manager, Date)

5. Define an action plan (who, what, when) to eliminate gaps and misalignments
6. Execute, evaluate, and adjust the action plan, as necessary

Wishing you much success in your pursuit of excellence in organizational performance and transformation, thereby generating greater value in your organization!

Strategy Maps

Clearly defined, communicated strategic direction and objectives are critical to the performance and success of an organization. A strategy map is an approach to define, document, communicate, and cascade the organization's strategies. It is a graphical diagram, which was presented by Robert S. Kaplan and David P. Norton in the mid 1990s, in association with the Balanced Scorecard.

A strategy map may be developed and deployed – for a corporation, business, function, or department – to set and communicate strategic objectives. It may be developed, then cascaded, from the top-level of an organization, with each subsequent level having a strategy map and scorecards supporting the next level up. Robert S. Kaplan said, "Process improvement programs are like teaching people *how* to fish. Strategy maps and scorecards teach people *where* to fish."

Benefits of using a strategy map include:

- Provide an approach to ensure strategies are successful
- Provide input for selecting initiatives and projects

Section 1: Strategic Approach

- Provide input for developing balanced and cascading scorecards
- Increase focus on the organization's strategies and attention on supporting metrics
- Provide a consistent approach for defining, documenting, and communicating strategic objectives

Sections and supporting elements of a strategy map may include:

Header

- **Purpose** – why the organization exists
- **Vision** – where the organization wants to be in the future
- **Mission** – how the organization will work toward its vision

Body and Strategy Map Categories

- **Finance** – financial strategic objectives
- **Customer** – customer strategic objectives
- **Internal Processes** – internal process strategic objectives
- **Learning and Growth** – learning and growth strategic objectives
    - Customized strategy maps may use variations of the four categories listed above
    - A lane or row on the strategy map is defined for each category
    - Each category will typically consist of three to five strategic objectives
    - Strategic objectives support and flow to the next higher lane on the strategy map

Footer

- **Values** – key and core values

While your strategy map may vary slightly, it will likely contain many of the components found in the following example depicting a basic strategy map, along with its elements.

Section 1: Strategic Approach

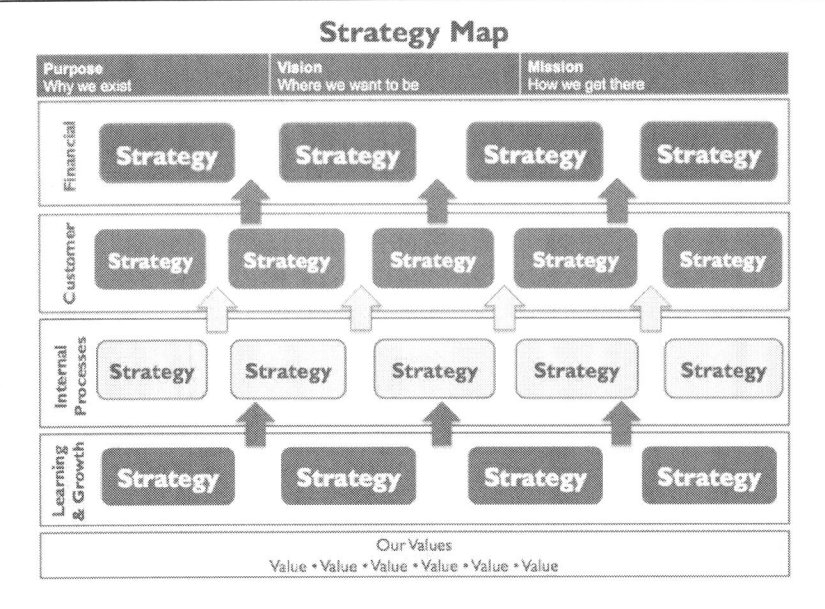

Strategy Map

Purpose	Vision	Mission
Why we exist	Where we want to be	How we get there

Financial: Strategy | Strategy | Strategy | Strategy

Customer: Strategy | Strategy | Strategy | Strategy | Strategy

Internal Processes: Strategy | Strategy | Strategy | Strategy | Strategy

Learning & Growth: Strategy | Strategy | Strategy | Strategy

Our Values
Value • Value • Value • Value • Value • Value

Strategy Map Process:

1. Assemble a team of participants who are briefed and come prepared to engage in the strategy map session
2. Define the organization's purpose, vision, mission, and values
3. Define organization-specific categories, or use the four standard categories described above
   a. Create an organization-level SIPOC with critical-to-customer (CTC) requirements
   b. Conduct an organization SWOT analysis for which the strategy map will represent
4. Define three to five strategic objectives for each category
   a. Conduct a force field analysis for each strategic objective
   b. Develop scorecards for each strategic objective
   c. Define initiatives or projects for each strategic objective
5. Document sections and elements of the strategy map
6. Execute, communicate, manage, cascade, and measure each strategy map and supporting strategic objectives

Strategy Map Process

Assemble a team → Define strategic objectives → Document the strategy map → Execute and measure the strategy map

Define purpose, vision, mission, and values → Define strategy map categories

Section 1: Strategic Approach

A strategy map may be used as input to cascading and balanced scorecards, as well as project selection and prioritization. While progress on strategic objectives should be managed, measured, and communicated regularly, they should be reassessed, revised, and communicated on an annual basis as part of the planning process.

Wishing you much success in your pursuit of executing strategic objectives, thereby generating greater value in your organization!

Prioritizing and Correlating Projects to Strategies

In today's fast-pace environment, resources and time are limited, and competition is fierce. Choosing the "right" improvement projects is crucial to the execution and achievement of the strategic goals. The flow-down process from strategic goals to the critical-few projects is an excellent way to ensure that resources are working on the right things.

The flow-down process starts with clearly defined top-level strategic direction, purpose, vision, mission, and values translated into short- and long-term strategic goals. The strategic goals are defined in terms of a strategy map and take into account many factors, including the voice of the business, voice of the customer, voice of the processes, and voice of the employees.

Once strategic goals are developed, the next step is to define associated programs and value streams necessary to identify potential improvement projects required to achieve these strategic goals. Through mapping and interrogating the current-state processes and value streams, then developing future-state processes and value streams, many potential projects are identified.

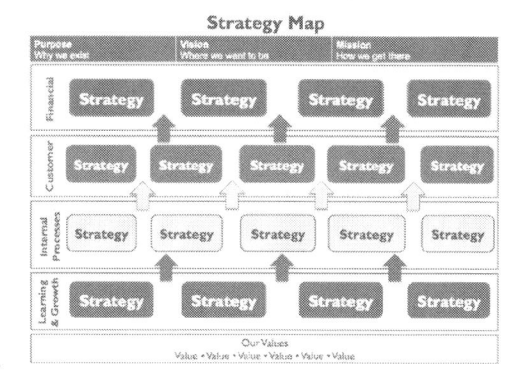

Section 1: Strategic Approach

Note that potential projects are evaluated and prioritized against specific criteria in three categories – impact, effort, and risk. Below is an example of a scheme for scoring potential projects; it may be used as a reference tool.

VALUE GENERATION PARTNERS — Project Scoring Scheme

Selection Criteria		Score 0	Score 1	Score 3	Score 5
Impact	Finance	No	Supports	Enables	Yes
	Customer	No	Supports	Enables	Yes
	Internal Processes	No	Supports	Enables	Yes
	Learning and Growth	No	Supports	Enables	Yes
Effort	People Resources		Low	Medium	High
	Budget Resources		In Plan	ROI	Out of Plan
	Duration of Project		<4 Mths	>4<12 Mths	>12 Mths
Risk	Technical Risk within the Project		Low	Medium	High
	Management Risk within the Project		Low	Medium	High

Enter potential projects into a project prioritization matrix, and enter a score for each element of each category. Total impact, effort, and risk, along with overall score and ranking, are auto-calculated by the template. Your project prioritization template may vary slightly, yet it will likely contain many of the components found in the following example.

VALUE GENERATION PARTNERS — Project Prioritization Matrix

Facilitator: _____   Date: _____

#	Project Description	Impact: Finance 25%	Customer 25%	Internal Processes 25%	Learning and Growth 25%	Total Impact 100%	Effort: People Resources 50%	Capital Resources 20%	Duration of Project 30%	Total Effort 100%	Risk: Technical Risk 40%	Management Risk 60%	Total Risk 100%	Impact × Effort ÷ Risk = Score (Variable weightings)	Rank
1															
2															
3															
4															
5															
6															
7															

Once prioritized, top-priority projects are correlated – in the Strategy Correlation Matrix – to the strategic goals, to validate complete coverage of the goals and to ensure alignment. While your strategy

Section 1: Strategic Approach

correlation matrix template may vary slightly, it will likely contain many of the components found in the following example.

			Strategies			
Facilitator:					Date:	
			Finance	Customer	Internal Processes	Learning & Growth
			Strategy / Strategy / Strategy	Strategy / Strategy / Strategy	Strategy / Strategy / Strategy	Strategy / Strategy / Strategy
Programs/Projects	Financial	Program/Project				
		Program/Project				
		Program/Project				
	Customer	Program/Project				
		Program/Project				
		Program/Project				
	Internal Processes	Program/Project				
		Program/Project				
		Program/Project				
	Learning & Growth	Program/Project				
		Program/Project				
		Program/Project				

Selected improvement projects – on which your organization will be engaging – are then chartered with goals, deliverables, in scope/out of scope, sponsors, project leads, team members, and high-level timelines. Each project has a kick-off call or meeting, followed by scheduled project report-outs and health-indicator (scope, schedule, and budget) reviews.

Project's health and successful execution are leading indicators to achieving strategic goals. For each strategic goal, a scorecard is developed and managed to ensure top-level strategic direction is being achieved.

Wishing you much success in your pursuit of operational excellence through project selection and execution, thereby generating greater value in your organization!

Section 1: Strategic Approach

Balanced and Cascading Scorecards

From George Odiorne to Peter Drucker, the quote, "If you can't measure something, you can't manage it," has been discussed, spoken, and written in many forms over the years. Regardless of how the quote is written, you need scorecards if you are to measure, manage, and improve your business, operations, and processes. This chapter suggests that you should consider developing and deploying balanced and cascading scorecards. Chuck Coonradt is well known for using cascading scorecards in his methodology, "The Game of Work." Robert Kaplan and David Norton are authors of "The Balanced Scorecard" and are credited with the balanced scorecard concept.

Below are benefits of balanced and cascading scorecards:

- Support appropriate project selection and prioritization
- Alignment of the organization toward common strategic objectives
- Support execution of strategic objectives
- Ensure correct and appropriate metrics are measured and managed
- Provide linkage between metrics and performance
- Support organizational understanding of strategic priorities and progress

Balanced and cascading scorecards start with the top-level position in the organization (Level One) and flow through all other levels, with focus on measuring and managing the critical few business results. It is important to consider that what you measure drives specific behavior. Selecting a Key Performance Indicator (KPI) that drives the wrong behavior may be much worse than having no scorecard at all. Balancing the scorecards across Financial, Customer, Internal Processes, and Learning and Growth categories supports strategic initiatives and ensures focus is given across the critical areas of the business. Another consideration is that each scorecard must be in alignment with vertical-level scorecards (scorecards in the organizationally hierarchical cascade) and the horizontal-level scorecards (scorecards of internal customers and suppliers to each position).

Section 1: Strategic Approach

So, where should you start? Start with a clear understanding of your organization's vision and strategic objects. Then, work with the Level One leader to select critical business metrics to monitor on scorecards – those that will drive organizational performance necessary to achieve strategic objectives as defined by the organizational strategy maps. Deploy these top-level scorecards by making them clearly understood and visible to the entire organization.

Now, progressing to direct reports of the top-level position, work with each Level Two leaders to define and deploy their critical scorecards. During this process, in order to secure ownership and sustainability, it is critical to work directly with those who will own the scorecards (Level Two leaders) and their leader – Level One. And then this is done at each level in the organization. Once each level of scorecards is developed, communicated, and made visible to the entire organization, progress toward strategic success will become visible; improvement efforts and directional changes then may be implemented, where necessary.

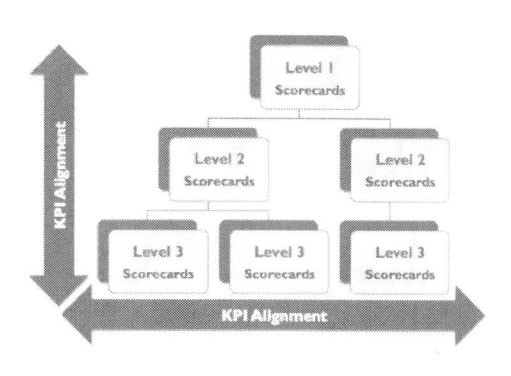

Each scorecard should include specific and common information:

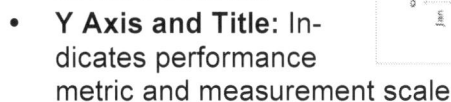

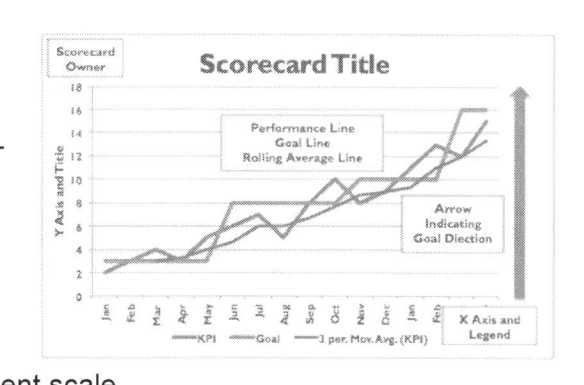

- **Title:** Descriptive of the scorecard metric and intent
- **Owner:** Clearly identified, responsible for timely updates, and accountable for performance results
- **Y Axis and Title:** Indicates performance metric and measurement scale
- **Performance Line:** Indicates actual and real-time performance of scorecard's KPI
- **Goal Line:** Achievable and adjusted, as goals are met and new

Section 1: Strategic Approach

standards are set
- **Rolling Average Line:** Indicates short-term performance
- **Directional Arrow:** Indicates the direction – up or down – expected for improvement
- **X Axis:** Indicates the time period between data points
- **Legend:** Identifies each line in the scorecard

An additional consideration for implementing balanced and cascading scorecards includes determining the actual number of scorecards necessary for each level and position. Often this is dependent on the level of the position and the position's direct impact on business-level results. Note: The Level One leader may have several scorecards, while a Level Six individual contributor may have one or two scorecards. Scorecards are most effective when reviewed in weekly coaching sessions. Balanced and cascading scorecards typically measure outputs or results. When the results are not as planned, the rigor and methodologies of A3 Thinking, PDCA, or Lean Six Sigma DMAIC are effective to understand and improve inputs that drive business results tracked on scorecards.

Wishing you much success in your pursuit of management by measurement through developing and deploying balanced and cascading scorecards, thereby generating greater value in your organization!

Quality Management System

One key element to achieving a successful operational excellence initiative is a well-defined and well-executed quality management system (QMS). A quality management system consists of a documented, communicated, prescribed, audited, reviewed, and revised set of policies, procedures, processes, objectives, and measures for organizational quality.

Your customers and/or industry may necessitate compliance to a specific quality management standard. However, the ISO 9000 quality management system series (ISO 9001 and ISO 9004) provides the foundational elements of a quality management system necessary to support an operational excellence-based organization. ISO 9001:2015 *Quality management systems – Requirements*, to be re-

Section 1: Strategic Approach

leased in late 2015, is the latest version of the standard, which was first published in 1987 by the International Organization for Standardization.

The ISO 9001 standard consists of eight sections, as listed below, with interactions depicted in the following image:

Section 1: Scope – overview of the standard and how it applies
Section 2: Normative Reference – indicates that ISO 9000 is a reference document
Section 3: Terms and Definitions – provides definitions of terms used in the standard
Section 4: Quality Management System – describes general requirements for a quality management system, including quality manual, procedures, forms, records, and document control
Section 5: Management Responsibility – describes top management's role in the quality management system, including commitment to develop, implement, improve, and review the QMS
Section 6: Resource Management – describes resource planning and work environment necessary to perform the function safely, continually improve, and satisfy the customer
Section 7: Product Realization – describes requirements for design, development, delivery, and service of a product or service, based on customer needs
Section 8: Measurement, Analysis, and Improvement – describes requirements for measuring, analyzing, and improving the quality management system using internal audits, monitoring customer satisfaction, and utilizing corrective and preventive action

Section 1: Strategic Approach

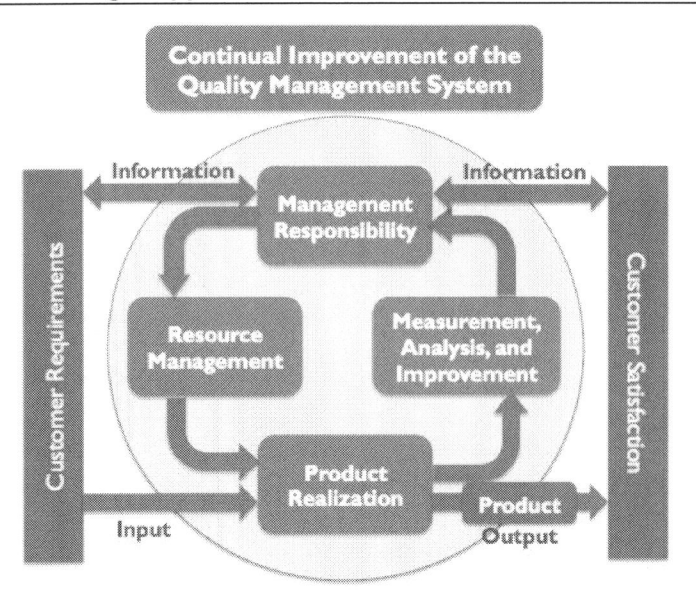

The ISO 9000 series is based on eight quality management principles, as listed below, and defined in ISO 9000:2005, *Quality management systems – Fundamentals and vocabulary* and ISO 9004:2009, *Managing for the sustained success of an organization – A quality management approach*.

1. **Customer focus** – understanding customer needs, meeting customer requirements, and striving to exceed customer expectations
2. **Leadership** – creating an environment of involvement; meeting objectives with unified purpose and direction
3. **Involvement of people** – throughout the entire organization
4. **Process approach** – efficiently and effectively achieve desired results
5. **System approach to management** – achieve objectives by managing related processes as systems
6. **Continual improvement** – performance of an organization as an ongoing objective
7. **Factual approach to decision making** – based on data and information analysis
8. **Mutually beneficial supplier relationships** – enhance value creation for both

Section 1: Strategic Approach

Documentation of a quality management system is typically based on four tiers, as described below, and depicted in a quality documentation pyramid:

1. **Policy manual**: Top-tier documentation; includes quality policy statement, quality policies, information on quality-related processes, listing and location of second-tier documentation, and reference standard for quality management system basis
2. **Procedures**: Second-tier documentation; includes controlled documents describing step-by-step standard operating procedures and detail at a process level
3. **Work instructions**: Third-tier documentation; includes controlled documents describing step-by-step instructions and detail at the task level
4. **Forms and records**: Fourth-tier documentation; includes outputs and evidence of executing the procedures and work instructions

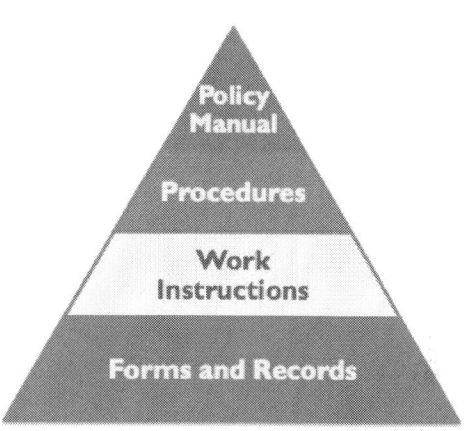

A quality management system typically consists of four facets:

- **Quality planning** – process of translating quality policy into processes, procedures, and instructions to achieve measurable objectives and requirements
- **Quality assurance** – planned and methodical activities executed as part of a quality system to provide confidence that process, product, or service requirements for quality are being satisfied
- **Quality control** – act of monitoring, appraising, and correcting a process, product, or service to ensure requirements for quality are being satisfied

Section 1: Strategic Approach

- **Quality improvement** – process of analyzing performance and taking methodical, systemic actions to improve it

Benefits of implementing a quality management system include:

- Provide a collaborative team environment
- Provide improved processes, products, and services
- Provide improved organizational efficiency and effectiveness
- Provide improved customer satisfaction
- Provide improved conformance and compliance
- Provide improved employee engagement and organizational culture

Wishing you much success in your pursuit of a quality management system, thereby generating greater value in your organization!

Section 2: Cultural Leadership

Another key element of the operational excellence transformation is cultural leadership. This section of the handbook includes chapters related specifically to proven practices for building a culture of leadership.

- Change Leadership
- Conflict Resolution
- Consensus Building
- Motivating Individuals
- Team Building

Please consider these as essential ingredients to successful cultural leadership supporting the value generation journey.

Change Leadership

Remaining competitive in today's global environment means organizations must be nimble and able to quickly implement change in strategy, structure, or technology, and adapt to these changes effectively. Changing a current-state organization to a desired future-state organization requires solid competency in integrated change leadership. Change leadership is the act of leading and managing change; it is critical to the success of any operational excellence transformation or continuous improvement initiative, as well as to the overall health of a high-performance culture. Peter Drucker has been quoted as saying, "The greatest danger in times of turbulence is not the turbulence; it is to act with yesterday's logic."

Most operational excellence transformation and continuous improvement initiatives fail to deliver desired results due to the absence of many of these critical change leadership elements:

- Leadership support, involvement, visibility
- Focus on and commitment to the initiative
- Clearly communicated and understood:
    o Vision and reason

Section 2: Cultural Leadership

- - Goals and expectations
  - Details and plans
  - Benefits and impacts to groups and individuals
- Sponsorship support at all phases of the initiative
- Qualified, capable project team managing all aspects of the initiative
- Application of project management rigor, discipline, and other appropriate methodologies
- Availability of necessary human, financial, and technological resources
- Adoption plan with extensive organizational involvement
- Training and skill development plan
- Measuring and monitoring results
- Adjusting, as necessary
- Recognition and celebration of success

Considerations for leading change:

- Lead by example
- Communicate, communicate, communicate
- Balance needs of individuals with those of the organization
- Provide vision, direction, and focus, yet allow individual freedom
- Gain support for the initiative from all groups impacted and from all levels of leadership
- Monitor and measure the change; learn and adapt when problems arise
- The more complex the change, the more persistence and patience required
- Don't bypass the change process
- Adjust approach based on the complexity of the change

Benefits of change leadership include:

- Improved organizational effectiveness, compliance, and risk prevention
- Environment of skill development, learning, and personal growth
- Sense of belonging and employee engagement
- Silos and barriers do not exist
- Better and more inclusive understanding of the organization

Section 2: Cultural Leadership

- Inclusive, collaborative environment in which individuals with diverse experience, skills, and backgrounds work toward common goals

Depicted in the following image, you will notice three groups to consider during the change leadership process; they are:

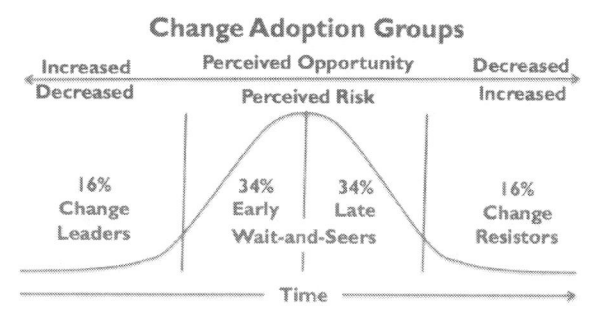

- **Change leaders** – those who will assist in leading change because they perceive significant opportunity with little associated risk
- **Wait-and-seers** – those who will change when they begin to see evidence that opportunity is increasing and risk is decreasing; this is the largest group of approximately 68 percent of individuals
- **Change resistors** – those who will resist change because they perceive little opportunity with significant risk

The change adoption curve defines phases, impact, feelings, and adjustments individuals and groups go through when faced with change. Based on work by psychiatrist and journalist Elisabeth Kübler-Ross, the change adoption curve depicts four phases, which are necessary to understand and manage when leading a successful change initiative.

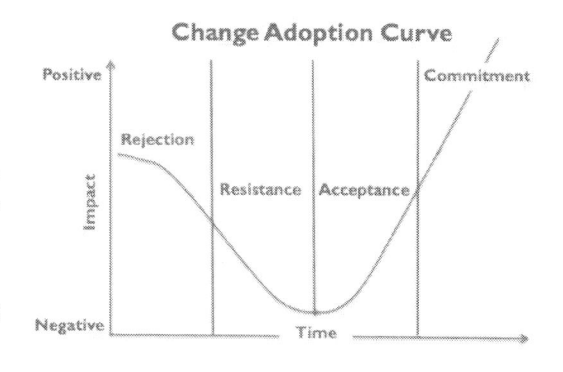

1. **Rejection** – "This does not apply to me and, if I wait, it will go away"
2. **Resistance** – "This won't work and I'm going back to doing it my way - the old way"
3. **Acceptance** – "This looks like it might work and may be even better than the old way"

21

Section 2: Cultural Leadership

4. **Commitment** – "This way works much better than the old way, and it's how I do things now"

The intent is to understand and use the change adoption curve, along with a change adoption plan, to reduce implementation time. Doing so will also reduce the change's negative impact on the organization and individuals. It is important to note that each of the three change adoption groups will experience the four phases at different paces, and with varying degrees of impact.

Change Leadership Process:

1. Develop and communicate vision, reason, goals, expectations, plans, benefits, and impacts of the change initiative
2. Identify a change initiative sponsor
3. Identify and launch change initiative project team
    a. Create project toolbox and charter with clearly defined deliverables, goal, scope, and success criteria
    b. Create project plan, schedule, stakeholder management plan, risk management plan, communication plan, and training plan
4. Assess and plan the organization's readiness for change using the following template
    a. While your change readiness plan template may vary slightly, it will likely contain many of the components found in the following example; this image depicts a basic change readiness plan template, along with its elements

Section 2: Cultural Leadership

Change Readiness Plan

Change Initiative or Project Name:					
Project Manager:			Date:		
Change Description:					
Who	What			When	Other
Owner	Readiness Element	Required	Status	Date	Comments
	Leadership support, involvement, and visibility				
	Communication plan				
	Vision - communicated and understood				
	Reason - communicated and understood				
	Expectations - communicated and understood				
	Impact - communicated and understood				
	Benefits - communicated and understood				
	Sponsor				
	Charter				
	Approach				
	Initiative/project leader				
	Initiative/project team resources				
	Financial resources				
	Technical resources				
	Adoption plan				
	Training and skill development plan				
	Measurements for success				
	Other as appropriate				

5. Execute the change initiative
   a. Inputs to the change initiative may include RACI matrix, process maps, SWOT analysis, force field analysis, etc.
   b. Create a change adoption plan using the template below
      i. While your change adoption plan template may vary slightly, it will likely contain many of the components found in the following example; this image depicts a basic change adoption plan template, along with its elements

Change Adoption Plan

Change Initiative or Project Name:								Project Manager:	
Change Description:									
Who			What		When	What	When		Other
Change Owner	Change Group	Stakeholder(s)	Resistance Level	Resistance Reason	Log Date	Adoption Strategy	Due Date	Adoption Status	Comments

6. Monitor, measure, and adjust based on the planned benefits and

Section 2: Cultural Leadership

    metrics for success
7. Acknowledge benefits and celebrate success of change implementation

Not all change initiatives are equal in complexity, nor do they require the same level of process to implement. Change initiatives will vary from those that are "just do it," to those that are full organizational transformations. Use the process level necessary for successfully implementing the change initiative based on an analysis of its complexity and impact on the organization and individuals. Note: "Just do it" initiatives will likely require scaled-down training and communication plans to ensure success.

	Change Process Level Applied Based on Change Initiative Complexity			
Example of Change Initiative	New Hire; Change to Process or Procedure	New Process, Product, or Service	Restructure; New Strategies; New Technology	Transformation; Acquisition; Merger
Process Level	Just Do It	Light Version	Medium Version	Full Version
Type of Engagement	Adapt		Adopt	

Wishing you much success in leading change, thereby generating greater value in your organization!

Conflict Resolution

Conflict is natural and inevitable. Organizations are comprised of individuals from diverse backgrounds, with varying experiences, skills, goals, and opinions. Conflict results from differences in motivations and opinions, expressed by emotional responses, such as frustration, fear, anger, and excitement. Any healthy, successful, and sustainable culture has conflict; it is normal behavior. Wellness author and speaker Greg Anderson is quoted as saying, "The Law of Win/Win says, 'Let's not do it your way or my way; let's do it the best way'."

Benefits of healthy conflict resolution include:

- Provide a collaborative team environment

Section 2: Cultural Leadership

- Provide an environment where silos and barriers do not exist
- Increase focus and attention on a sustainable, healthy culture
- Establish a culture where the expectation is to respectfully, constructively resolve issues
- Provide an inclusive environment in which individuals with diverse experience, skills, and backgrounds work together on common goals

It is helpful to recognize symptoms of conflict, and more importantly, to determine and eliminate – or prevent – actual causes of conflict.

Symptoms of conflict include:

- Impatience with other team members
- Mistrust and lack of understanding
- Arguing; defending positions and ideas
- Ideas and suggestions are unconnected; not building on others' ideas and suggestions
- Distortion of facts and information to support personal agendas

Causes of conflict include:

- Threats to status and organizational structure
- Pressures from roles, responsibilities
- Differences in perceptions, values
- Differences in standards
- Clashes in motivations, behaviors
- Inconsistencies in priorities, goals
- Changes in processes, procedures

Considerations for preventing conflict:

- Appreciate limitations of arguing and debating
- Believe that ideas and solutions can be mutually acceptable
- Understand that conflict is a natural, healthy element of decision making
- Acknowledge that differences in ideas are useful and lead to creative solutions
- Openness to others' ideas and suggestions, with a willingness to examine possibilities

Section 2: Cultural Leadership

- Recognizing that some of the best ideas and solutions are generated through conflict resolution

Conflict Resolution Process:

1. Bring together conflicting parties; select a comfortable and neutral environment
2. Identify conflict source and root cause
3. Define potential solutions to cause of conflict
4. Develop mutual agreement on an acceptable solution to the conflict
5. Define a plan to implement mutually agreed-upon solution
6. Execute, evaluate, and adjust the solution plan, as necessary

Conflict Resolution Process

- Bring parties together
- Identify source and root cause
- Define potential solutions
- Mutually agree on a solution
- Define plan to implement
- Execute, evaluate, and adjust

Considerations for resolving conflict:

- Encourage participants to propose and select the best solution
- Determine how important the issue is to all participants
- Listen carefully to each person's point of view; separate areas of agreement from disagreement
- Ask participants how the process may be improved; evaluate costs versus gains
- Ensure all parties understand their responsibilities, including dealing with the problem and the solution

Tools and techniques useful for conflict resolution include:

- Cause-and-effect matrix
- Decision tree
- Fault tree analysis
- Force field analysis
- Impact/effort matrix
- Pairwise comparison
- Six thinking hats
- Solution-selection matrix

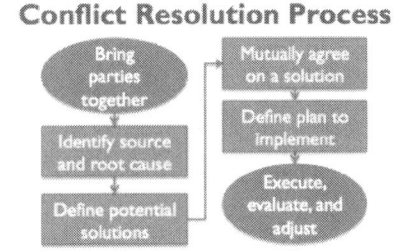

Section 2: Cultural Leadership

Wishing you much success in resolving conflict in a healthy, constructive manner, thereby generating greater value in your organization!

Consensus Building

Building consensus is an essential behavior to integrate into the organization's culture; it is a key element ensuring ideas are supported and actions are executed with ownership and accountability. Consensus building is the resolution of conflict and disagreement in order to reach a collaborative agreement with solidarity and harmony. It is a group decision and collective agreement, which is supported and carried forward by the group. Martin Luther King, Jr. is quoted as saying, "A genuine leader is not a searcher for consensus, but a molder of consensus."

Merriam-Webster defines consensus as:

- A general agreement about something
- An idea or opinion that is shared by all people in a group
- A judgment arrived at by most of those concerned

Synonyms of consensus include accord, agreement, concurrence, harmony, and solidarity. Antonyms of consensus are conflict, disagreement, disunity, and discord.

Benefits of consensus building include:

- Provide a collaborative team environment
- Provide a consistent approach for making decisions
- Provide support and ownership of decisions
- Increase focus and attention on decision making

Consensus Building Process:

1. Assemble a team of participants who are briefed and come prepared to engage in the session
2. Define the topic, issue, problem of the session
3. Define session process and ground rules

Section 2: Cultural Leadership

4. Identify alternatives, such as solutions and options, to the session topic
5. Conduct decision-making process to formulate agreement and consensus
6. Carry the decision forward to the next step or phase

Consensus Building Process

Assemble a team → Identify alternatives → Conduct decision making → Carry decision forward
Define the session topic → Define process and ground rules

Elements of consensus building:

- It is not a win or lose situation
- Avoid debating and arguing over ideas
- Use ground rules established by the team
- State position with facts and respect
- Use proven facilitation tools and techniques
- Differences of opinion are natural and healthy; ensure they are stated in a respectful manner
- Involve the entire team in the decision-making process
- Ensure every member will support the decision
- No one leaves the session in silent disagreement

Tools and techniques useful for consensus building:

- Affinity diagram
- Brainstorming
- Cause-and-effect matrix
- Decision tree
- Fault tree analysis
- Force field analysis
- Impact/effort matrix
- Multivoting
- Nominal group technique
- Pairwise comparison
- Pugh matrix
- Six thinking hats
- Solution-selection matrix

I like to include a thumbs up/down/sideways technique when facilitating a team through this process. It allows all of the members to

Section 2: Cultural Leadership

participate in the decision in a visual manner, and it may lighten the mood and discussions during the process.

The "thumbs" approach goes as follows:

- Thumbs up – in complete agreement with the decision
- Thumbs down – in complete disagreement with the decision
- Thumbs sideways – not in total agreement, but will support the decision

Consensus is reached when all team members have either thumbs up or thumbs sideways positions, and any thumbs down positions have been resolved.

Wishing you much success in your pursuit of building consensus, thereby generating greater value in your organization!

Motivating Individuals

The most successful organizations are those that have a culture of motivated individuals who come together to form effective teams, accomplishing strategic goals and objectives set forth by the organization's leaders. And motivational leaders set the tone for such a culture. John Mackey, co-founder and co-CEO of Whole Foods Market, is quoted as saying, "If you are lucky enough to be someone's employer, then you have a moral obligation to make sure people do look forward to coming to work in the morning."

To motivate individuals, it is important to understand their needs. Effective leaders build and shape organizations that motivate their employees' minds, spirits, *and actions*. Cognitive evaluation theory (CET) of motivation indicates that there are two kinds of interconnected motivators to consider.

- **Intrinsic motivators** result from performance of an activity, including responsibility and achievement

Section 2: Cultural Leadership

- **Extrinsic motivators** result from environmental factors, including working conditions, pay, and performance evaluations

Intrinsic and extrinsic motivators are related to and impact each of these motivation theories.

- Alderfer's ERG Theory
- Herzberg's Two-Factor Theory
- Maslow's Hierarchy of Needs
- McClelland's Acquired Needs Theory

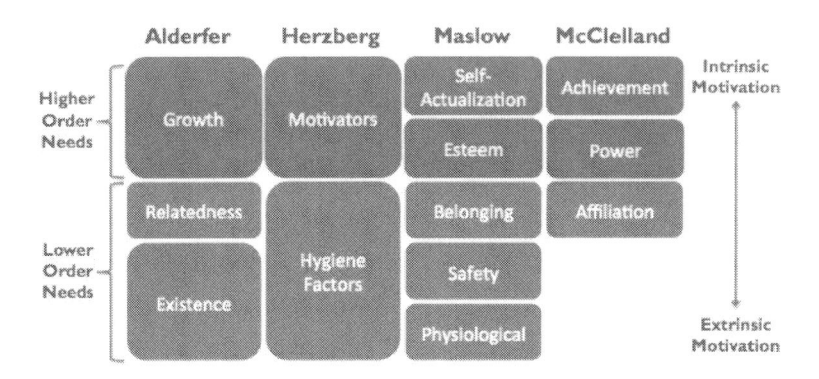

	Alderfer	Herzberg	Maslow	McClelland	
Higher Order Needs	Growth	Motivators	Self-Actualization	Achievement	Intrinsic Motivation
			Esteem	Power	
Lower Order Needs	Relatedness	Hygiene Factors	Belonging	Affiliation	
	Existence		Safety		
			Physiological		Extrinsic Motivation

Alderfer's ERG Theory:

Clayton Alderfer's ERG theory is formed on the basis of Maslow's Hierarchy of Needs, but collapses five levels into three categories – existence, relatedness, and growth.

- **Existence** – aspirations for material and physical well-being (includes Maslow's physiological and safety levels)
- **Relatedness** – aspirations for fulfilling relationships (includes Maslow's belonging and esteem levels)
- **Growth** – aspirations for development of capability, growth, or potential (includes Maslow's esteem and self-actualization levels)

Existence needs are considered the first level of needs and foundational to motivating behavior. As lower-level needs are satisfied, they become less important; as higher-level needs are satisfied, they become more important. To strive for a culture of motivation, leaders must ensure that individuals' lower-level needs are met (and thus no

Section 2: Cultural Leadership

longer important), so that individuals have opportunities to achieve higher-level needs, such as relatedness and growth.

Herzberg's Two-Factor Theory:

Just as its name describes, Fredrick Herzberg's Two-Factor Theory is based on the premise that motivation is divided into two factors.

- **Hygiene factors** include job security, salary or pay, benefits, policies, relationships, and working conditions. While these factors do not directly motivate individuals, when not present or when taken away, they cause dissatisfaction and complaints.
- **Motivators** include achievement, advancement, growth, responsibility, and a feeling of recognition. When present, these factors directly motivate and satisfy individuals; however, when they are not present, they do not dissatisfy.

The two factors have four combinations:

- High hygiene and high motivation – best situation; results in individuals who have few complaints and are highly motivated
- High hygiene and low motivation – results in individuals who have few complaints, yet are not highly motivated
- Low hygiene and high motivation – results in individuals who are dissatisfied, yet highly motivated
- Low hygiene and low motivation – worst situation; results in individuals who are dissatisfied and not motivated

Since absence of hygiene factors causes dissatisfaction and complaints, and motivators cause satisfaction and high motivation, leaders must ensure that hygiene factors are in place, and then strengthen individuals' opportunities to experience motivators.

Maslow's Hierarchy of Needs:

Abraham Maslow's Hierarchy of Needs defines a need as a physiological or psychological deficiency requiring satisfaction. While a satisfied need is not a motivator, an unsatisfied need influences behavior until fulfilled.

Section 2: Cultural Leadership

Maslow's Hierarchy of Needs is based on two principles:

- **Deficit principle** states that a satisfied need does not motivate behavior since individuals work to satisfy missing needs
- **Progression principle** states that the five needs occur in a hierarchy, meaning lower-level needs must be satisfied first

Maslow's hierarchy consists of five levels:

- **Physiological** – workplace, work hours, comfort
- **Safety** – pay, work conditions, benefits, job security
- **Belonging** – coworkers, teams, leaders, customers
- **Esteem** – status, respect, responsibility, promotion, praise, recognition
- **Self-Actualization** – challenge, flexibility, achievement, growth, opportunity, advancement, creativity

Maslow's Hierarchy of Needs suggests that the lower-level needs must be met before individuals will desire moving to higher-level needs. Leaders must recognize and understand the five levels of needs in order to build a culture of motivation within their organizations.

McClelland's Acquired Needs Theory:

David McClelland's Acquired Needs Theory acknowledges that individuals prioritize three specific needs differently.

- **Affiliation** – wish to form close, personal, friendly relationships
- **Power** – desire to be in charge; to control and influence others' actions
- **Achievement** – determination to accomplish something of importance; to excel

Leaders must build and shape an organization that maximizes its results and success based on recognizing and meeting individuals' needs.

Benefits of motivating individuals include:

- Reduce costs and turnover

Section 2: Cultural Leadership

- Increase individuals' satisfaction
- Increase quality, productivity, customer satisfaction
- Provide an environment to ensure strategies are successful
- Provide a collaborative environment and sense of belonging
- Increase success of organization's strategies and metrics
- Increase focus, attention, energy toward organizational goals

Motivation Cycle:

1. Recognize an individual's deficiency of needs
2. Collaborate with individual to define a plan to fulfill his/her needs
3. Execute plan to fulfill needs
4. Monitor individual's motivation level
5. Provide feedback to/solicit input from individual; adjust plan as necessary

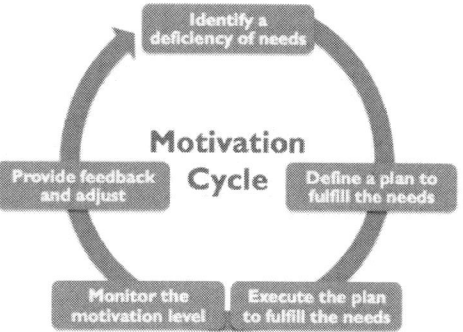

Although there is not a single, magical solution for motivating individuals, careful consideration of each of these theories and how they might be applied to build and shape a highly motivated organization will most certainly result in benefits and rewards to all.

Wishing you much success in your pursuit of motivating individuals, thereby generating greater value in your organization!

Team Building

Henry Ford, the founder of Ford Motor Company, delivered a clear and concise message regarding the importance of teams and the power of team building by saying, "Coming together is a beginning. Keeping together is progress. Working together is success." The strength and success of an organization's operational excellence transformation are highly dependent on a strong team culture.

Section 2: Cultural Leadership

A team consists of people with complementary skills who are committed to a common purpose, with action plans and a set of performance goals for which it takes ownership and holds itself accountable. You may consider an entire organization a team, with an overall culture, and each department and function within the organization a team with its own subculture. You may also form teams with specific goals, purposes, and durations, as described below:

- **Ad hoc** teams are formed with short notice, for a specific purpose, with a limited scope and short duration, and may be comprised of cross-functional members
- **Cross-functional** teams are multi-disciplined and multi-functional, typically focused on efforts, processes, operations, procedures, and deliverables; they may cross multiple departments or functions
- **Functional** teams are permanent teams formed within a department to focus on specific functions within the organization
- **Improvement** teams address quality, efficiency, productivity, or transformational opportunities; they may be comprised of cross-functional members
- **Leadership** teams are formed to include those members of the organization who have a strategic role and guide the organization to achieve the vision, mission, and strategies
- **Lean Six Sigma** teams focus on specific improvement processes and projects that require a reduction in variation and/or non-value-added activities; they may be comprised of cross-functional members
- **Project** teams work on specific initiatives that have defined deliverables, scope, and schedule to deliver a solution, such as a service, product, or other defined outcome; these teams may be comprised of cross-functional members
- **Quality** teams focus on quality-related opportunities and topics to address problems, improve performance, and achieve quality goals
- **Self-directed** teams are empowered to operate and authorized to deliver results without direction or supervision from management
- **Task forces** are comprised of experts with wide authority and decision-making freedom, formed for a specific purpose, which may be political or sensitive in nature; these teams may include cross-functional members
- **Virtual** teams are made up of members located in varying geo-

Section 2: Cultural Leadership

graphic locations; these teams use technological tools to interact, conduct meetings, and achieve goals

American industrialist and philanthropist Andrew Carnegie once said, "Teamwork is the ability to work together toward a common vision – the ability to direct individual accomplishments toward organizational objectives. It is the fuel that allows common people to attain uncommon results." Recognizing, understanding, and building on the stages of team development are critical to integrating a team culture into your organization. Psychologist Bruce Tuckman used the phrase "forming, storming, norming, and performing" in the article, <u>Development Sequence in Small Groups</u>, in 1965, to describe the process of group development in achieving high performance and delivering results.

Below are the four stages of team development:

Forming – members are typically excited, anxious, positive, and polite

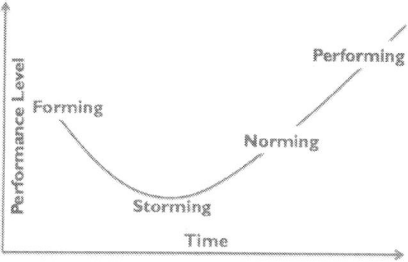

- Have a strong dependency on the leader
- Starting to work together and get to know each other
- Feeling uncertain about their roles within the team
- Not yet sure what is expected of them nor what they may contribute
- Beginning to understand goals, deliverables, processes, and procedures

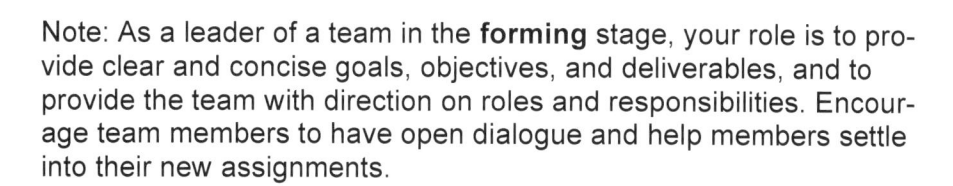

Note: As a leader of a team in the **forming** stage, your role is to provide clear and concise goals, objectives, and deliverables, and to provide the team with direction on roles and responsibilities. Encourage team members to have open dialogue and help members settle into their new assignments.

Storming – members begin to think individually, have conflict, are distracted from the goals

- Loyalties are divided; leadership is challenged

Section 2: Cultural Leadership

- Teams engage in confrontation, disagreements, arguments, complaining
- Split into sub-groups due to lack of trust for other members and/or leader
- Question the approach, methods, processes being used
- Challenge support for the team; may begin to rebel

Note: As a leader of a team in the **storming** stage, it is necessary to take on a more directive role in order to establish structure, clearly define how the team will work together, and clarify roles and responsibilities. It is your responsibility to build trust, resolve conflict, address concerns, and provide resolutions amenable to all members. You must recognize and address when members revisit the storming stage, typically due to membership changes, goals changing, or leadership changes.

Norming – members start working together, have less conflict, focus on the goals

- Goals, deliverables, and approach are understood and supported by members
- Understand and accept their roles and responsibilities, as well as others' roles and responsibilities
- Begin to work together as a cohesive team; trust and collaboration exist
- Focus is switched from conflict and challenge to achieving goals

Note: As a leader of a team in the **norming** stage, your role is to co-ordinate the team's functions and activities at a high level, and to guide the team to take responsibility and manage toward the goal.

Performing – members begin to focus on the process, operate efficiently, achieve goals

- Trust, positive energy, motivation, enthusiasm
- Ownership and clarity of the goals, approach, activities, tasks
- Exhibit open dialogue and communications
- Knowledgeable, competent, able to manage decision-making process
- Rely on each other; collaborative, interdependent cooperation
- Handle conflict; reach consensus

Section 2: Cultural Leadership

Note: As a leader of a team in the **performing** stage, your role is to delegate much of the authority and decision making to the team; focus your efforts on developing team members.

Adjourning is a fifth stage (for non-permanent teams), added by Tuckman in 1977, to identify when the work is complete and the team is dissolved. As a leader of a team in the adjourning stage, your role is to ensure team evaluations are complete, help members transition off the team and into another role, and celebrate the success of the team's accomplishments.

Benefits of building effective teams include:

- Environment of skill development and learning
- Approach for personal growth and satisfaction
- Collaborative environment; sense of belonging
- Environment where silos and barriers do not exist
- Inclusive understanding of the organization
- Environment to efficiently and effectively resolve issues that individuals alone cannot resolve
- Diverse and inclusive environment in which individuals work toward common goals

T - Together
E - Everyone
A - Achieves
M - More

Characteristics of a *successful* team include members having:

- An understanding of their roles and responsibilities
- An understanding of their purpose and goals, as well as a documented plan for how to achieve those goals
- Participation in team discussions and decisions, and to share accountability and ownership of execution and results
- Respect for each other and a commitment to resolve conflicts
- Appropriate communication and listening skills
- A use of fact-based decision making with data and statistical analysis
- Effective and efficient meetings, with adherence to ground rules and suitable record keeping

Section 2: Cultural Leadership

Leadership's contribution to a team's success includes:

- Provide sense of purpose and mission
- Provide plan and goals with direction and support
- Share business results
- Reinforce positive outcomes

Characteristics of an *ineffective* team include:

- Unclear goals and objectives, with no plan or little documentation
- Unclear roles and responsibilities
- Dominating members force their ideas on others
- Members' ideas are ignored and actions are limited
- Lack of involvement and communication
- Making decisions on instinctive reaction, with no facts or data to support
- Blame, unresolved conflict, lack of trust
- Tangents, digression, lack of focus

Team Building Process:

1. Determine the type of team required, based on the goals and objectives
2. Assemble and launch the team
3. Conduct reviews to identify the team's stage of development
4. Determine appropriate actions to move the team to performing stage
5. Take action with team until performing stage is achieved
6. Once team's goals are achieved, adjourn the team and celebrate its success

Team Building Process

Determine team type → Define action → Assemble team → Take action → Review team → Adjourn and celebrate

Wishing you much success in your pursuit of building cohesive, well-functioning teams, thereby generating greater value in your organization!

Section 3:
Practices and Methodologies

A key element of the operational excellence transformation is rigorous and disciplined methodologies. This section of the handbook includes chapters related specifically to proven practices and methodologies used in business today to generate value for shareholders, customers, and companies.

- Facilitating Continuous Improvement Events
    - Improving Cross-Functional Processes
    - Finding and Eliminating Waste
    - Reducing Cost of Quality
- A3 PDCA, LSS DMAIC, and DfLSS DMADV
    - A3 Thinking
    - Lean Six Sigma (LSS) DMAIC
    - Design for Lean Six Sigma (DfLSS) DMADV
- Theory of Constraints (TOC)

Please consider these as essential ingredients to successful practices and methodical approaches supporting the value generation journey.

Facilitating Continuous Improvement Events

Facilitating continuous improvement events is an effective approach to managing and achieving short-term goals and objectives in a face-to-face, cross-functional environment. Continuous improvement events may be conducted for many purposes, such as process improvement, waste reduction, cost-of-quality reduction, project selection, and strategy development and deployment. Much thought and consideration must be given to planning and conducting continuous improvement events to ensure successful outcomes.

Facilitating continuous improvement events may be useful when:

- Quality levels are deteriorating and solutions are not readily

Section 3: Practices and Methodologies

available
- There are many and varying opinions on how to achieve a goal
- Goals and objectives must be completed in a short cycle time
- A customer is not receiving products or services as intended
- Team and cross-functional collaboration are necessary to ensure success
- It is necessary for a group to work in a face-to-face environment to achieve a goal
- Goals include waste reduction, cycle-time reduction, process improvement, or quality improvement

Benefits of facilitating continuous improvement events include:

- Provide a collaborative team environment
- Provide a consistent approach for facilitating events
- Increase focus and attention on customer satisfaction
- Save cost and time by rapid goal and objective achievement
- Increase focus and attention on continuous improvement efforts
- Provide an approach for efficiently and effectively conducting continuous improvement efforts

Process for Facilitating Continuous Improvement Events:

Pre-Event

1. Identify facilitator, sponsor, and key stakeholders
2. Facilitator and sponsor develop a continuous improvement event charter
    a. Event name
    b. Problem statement
    c. Goals, objectives, deliverables
    d. Timeline for completion of deliverables
    e. In-scope and out-of-scope statements
    f. Success criteria
    g. Issues, risks, dependencies
3. Facilitator and sponsor determine the event date, duration, location
4. Facilitator and sponsor identify event participants
5. Facilitator and sponsor conduct a kick-off call/meeting with event participants to describe
    a. Event purpose and deliverables

Section 3: Practices and Methodologies

      b. Participants' roles and responsibilities for before, during, and after the event
      c. Preparation and pre-work
6. Facilitator provides participants with pre-work on the event topic
7. Facilitator secures an event location and event supplies
      a. Butcher block paper, flip charts, Post-it® notes, markers, tape, digital projector, etc.
8. Facilitator arrives at the event location in advance to ensure appropriate set-up and preparation
      a. U-shape room arrangement, refreshments (water, coffee, snacks, etc.), event supplies, etc.

<u>Event</u>

9. Sponsor and facilitator kick-off the event
      a. Problem, goal, objective, scope, etc.
      b. Introductions, expectations, concerns, ground rules
      c. Participant roles and responsibilities
      d. Agenda items, time, duration
      e. Facilities, snacks, lunches, etc.
10. Participants define and document the current (as-is) process where the problem is located
      a. May develop a SIPOC, RACI, flowchart, input/output map, or deployment flowchart
      b. May conduct a SWOT analysis
11. Participants list issues within the current-state process, which likely cause the problem
      a. May conduct silent brainstorming, create an affinity diagram, or facilitate mind mapping
12. Participants prioritize issues with current-state process
      a. May use multi-voting or pairwise comparison
13. Participants determine the cause of the prioritized issues
      a. May use cause-and-effect diagram, cause-and-effect matrix, and 5 Why
14. Participants define and document a future-state (to-be or ideal) process, which eliminates the issues within the current-state process
      a. May develop a SIPOC, RACI, flowchart, input/output map, or deployment flowchart
      b. May use solution-selection matrix or Pugh matrix
      c. May create an impact/effort matrix or force field analysis
      d. May conduct FMEA

Section 3: Practices and Methodologies

15. Participants define an action plan to implement the future-state process
    a. Identify an owner of the action plan
    b. Identify an action plan implementation team – who, what, and when
        i. Define a close-out plan and timeline
        ii. Define a communication plan, training plan, and control plan
16. Participants conduct an event report-out with the sponsor and key stakeholders
    a. Participants, not the facilitator, present the report-out
    b. Secure approval to proceed with the action plan

<u>Post-Event</u>

17. Process owner conducts weekly team update calls on action plan assignments
18. Process owner and team conduct sponsor updates based on the communication plan
19. Owner conducts a close-out call with the sponsor
20. Owner and sponsor conduct a close-out celebration with the team

Wishing you much success in your pursuit of continuous improvement, thereby generating greater value in your organization!

Improving Cross-Functional Processes

Are your processes fully documented – including listing your suppliers, customers, and critical-to-customer (CTC) characteristics? Do your employees know their roles and responsibilities within your processes? If not, I hope you find value in this chapter, which is intended to guide you through the use of three simple tools to document and improve cross-functional processes.

It is interesting how many times I hear folks say, "We don't have a process for that." In turn, I ask if they have performed the steps necessary to get the output, and the response is always "yes." If it is "yes," then there is a process, yet it is simply not documented. So let us consider these basic tools for documenting current processes –

Section 3: Practices and Methodologies

SIPOC, Swimlane Map, and RACI Matrix. I use these three tools the most for documenting current state and planning for future-state processes.

1. Start by documenting the process by using **SIPOC** (**S**uppliers – **I**nputs – **P**rocess – **O**utputs – **C**ustomers). A completed SIPOC includes a list of the suppliers to the process, the inputs to the process, the process itself, outputs of the process, and a list of customers of the process. Note: Included in my SIPOC is an additional column, titled "CTC," or Critical-To-Customer; it contains a list of the critical-to-customer characteristics expected *from* the process *by* the customer *of* the process.

\multicolumn{6}{c}{SIPOC Layout}
Suppliers	**Inputs**	**Process**	**Outputs**	**Customers**	**CTCs**
List the suppliers to the process	List the inputs to the process as provided by the suppliers	Define the process	List the outputs of the process	List the customers of the process	List the critical to customer characteristics

2. Follow the SIPOC by defining a **Swimlane Map** of the process, which is ideal for documenting processes that cross multiple functions or departments. Swimlane maps include a "lane" for each function or department involved in the process. The beginning of the process and its end are the mapping boundaries for the entire map; the flow of the process is documented as process steps, handoffs, decision points, and loop backs through various swimlanes.

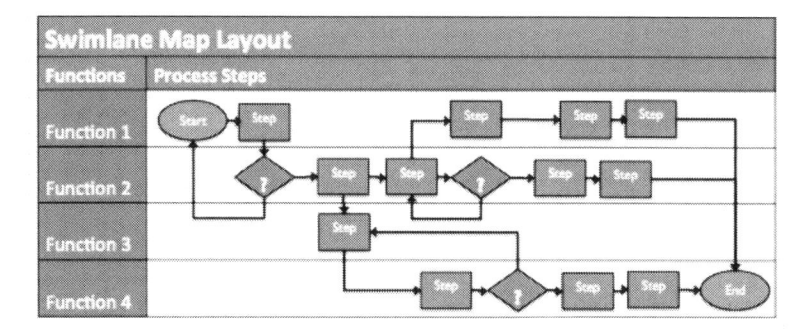

Swimlane Map Layout	
Functions	**Process Steps**
Function 1	Start → Step → Step → Step → Step
Function 2	? → Step → Step → ? → Step → Step
Function 3	Step
Function 4	Step → ? → Step → Step → End

3. After creating the SIPOC and Swimlane Map, you will define a **RACI** (**R**esponsible, **A**ccountable, **C**onsulted, and **I**nformed) **Ma-**

Section 3: Practices and Methodologies

trix for the process. A RACI Matrix is used to document the roles and responsibilities associated within the process. In this example of a RACI matrix layout, list the names of the swimlanes across the top, and list the process steps down the left side. The center of the RACI matrix is used to correlate the process steps with the roles or swimlane names. Then, simply assign "R" for the role or function that is responsible for the process step, "A" for the role or function that is accountable for the process step, "C" for whom must be consulted during the process step, and "I" for whom must be informed of the process step.

RACI Matrix Layout

Functions	Function 1	Function 2	Function 3	Function 4
Process Step	A	R	C	C
Process Step	R	A	I	I
Process Step	A	R	I	I
Process Step	C	I	R	A
Process Step	C	I	A	R
Process Step	A	I	I	R
Process Step	I	C	R	A

Before starting to document your process, identify the subject matter experts (SMEs) needed to help you complete accurate documentation. Schedule your mapping session. Assign the Process SMEs pre-work of sketching their version of the current process. Facilitate the mapping session by completing a SIPOC, Swimlane Map, and RACI Matrix. Note: It is very helpful to add titles, owners, and revision dates to each process document.

Now that you have your current-state process documented, you can use this documentation as a training aid or a starting point for process improvement initiatives. As a training aid, you might post the documents on your internal website or network, as well as posting at the point of use. Follow the process improvement cycle below to document and improve cross-functional processes.

Process Improvement Cycle:

1. Document the current-state process (SIPOC, Swimlane Map, and RACI)

Section 3: Practices and Methodologies

2. Evaluate the current-state process looking for issues and opportunities for continuous improvement, such as
   a. Missing control points
   b. Duplication of efforts and tasks
   c. Sources of errors
   d. Unnecessary tasks and non-value-added activities
   e. Loop backs, decision points, and handoffs
   f. Illogical or inefficient sequencing of tasks
   g. Unclear lines of responsibility
   h. Standards that are no longer used
3. Define a future-state process, which eliminates issues and leverages opportunities identified in current-state process
4. Develop an implementation action plan, including *who, what,* and *when* to implement the new future-state process
5. Manage and control the future-state process
6. Rerun the process improvement cycle looking for new continuous improvement opportunities

An example of using these tools to improve a cross-functional process is a project team challenged with reducing the order-to-cash cycle time within a bicycle manufacturer. The team documents the current order-to-cash process using SIPOC, swimlane map, and RACI. The current process documentation is analyzed for issues, such as decision points, loop backs, redundant responsibilities, delays, and handoffs. A new process is defined to eliminate issues and reduce cycle time.

Traditional problem-solving approaches analyze and fix outputs, without addressing the inputs and sources of waste; continuous improvement is an iterative process that focuses on minimizing variation and eliminating waste to bring products and services ever closer to customers' changing needs. Regardless of your purpose for engaging in this exercise, it is an excellent way to generate value for your organization by clearly documenting and improving your current processes using three simple tools described earlier. As in any effort or initiative, one must always be on the lookout for the potential to

Section 3: Practices and Methodologies

jeopardize the overall process through isolated improvements. Approach these process improvement initiatives with the overall process in mind, as well as the organization's strategy and culture.

Wishing you much success in your pursuit of documenting and improving your processes, thereby generating greater value in your organization!

Finding and Eliminating Waste

It is well known that there are eight types of waste that are present in most processes and in all industries. The trick is to be able to identify the waste, and determine and eliminate the cause. Below is a list of the eight types of waste. Notice the acronym **TIM U WOOD**; it is an easy way to remember these eight types of waste.

- **T**ransportation or Conveyance: Movement of materials, products, or services
- **I**nventory: Excess supplies or materials requiring unnecessary storage
- **M**otion: Movement by employees that does not add value to the product or service

- **U**nder Utilization of People or Talent: Not engaging or listening to employees

- **W**aiting or Delays: Idle time while waiting for materials or information
- **O**ver Production: Producing more or sooner than needed
- **O**ver Processing: Extra steps in the process that are not necessary
- **D**efects: Doing work incorrectly or reworking a product or service

A second acronym that is helpful to remember the eight forms of waste is **DOWNTIME**.

- **D**efects
- **O**ver Production
- **W**aiting

Section 3: Practices and Methodologies

- **N**on-Utilized Talent
- **T**ransportation
- **I**nventory
- **M**otion
- **E**xtra Processing

Ideally your information, products, or services flow through a process with no waste.

Waste Elimination Cycle:

1. Identify your customers and what they value
2. Identify non-value-added (waste) activities in your processes, engaging in process-mapping work; once you have an eye for the flow, you will not be able to look at a process without seeing its associated waste
3. Determine the root cause of the waste; simple methods for finding the root cause of waste are to employ techniques known as Cause-and-Effect and 5 Why; list all of the potential causes of the waste, and then simply ask why a particular waste exists until you have determined the root cause; while the technique is called 5 Why, it may take fewer – or more – than five whys to find the true or actionable root cause, in order to eliminate the waste
4. Once the root cause of waste is identified, it is effective to engage in brainstorming techniques to determine, evaluate, and select solutions for new processes – thus removing the causes of waste; the next step is to define an action plan consisting of who is responsible for the action, what the action consists of, and when the action will be completed
5. Monitor the execution of the action plan to ensure dates are met and the expected results are realized; include controls in the action plan to sustain benefits of the gains
6. Rerun the waste-elimination cycle looking for new continuous improvement opportunities

Section 3: Practices and Methodologies

While there are more involved approaches, such as value-stream mapping, this approach will teach employees to participate in simple daily improvements.

Traditional problem-solving approaches analyze and fix the outputs, without addressing the inputs and sources of waste; continuous improvement is an iterative process that focuses on minimizing variation and eliminating waste to bring products and services ever closer to customers' changing needs. Regardless of your purpose for engaging in this exercise, it is an excellent way to generate value for your organization by eliminating waste from your processes. As in any effort or initiative, one must always be on the lookout for the potential to jeopardize the overall process through isolated improvements. Approach these process improvement initiatives with the overall process in mind, as well as the organization's strategy and culture.

Wishing you much success in your pursuit of waste elimination, thereby generating greater value in your organization!

Reducing Cost of Quality

It is well known – or is it? – that most quality costs are hidden "below the surface." Studies have shown that as much as 30 percent of revenues may go to cost of quality. Referring to the iceberg image, you will notice that the majority of the iceberg is below the waterline. Equating this to business, it translates into approximately five percent of quality cost is visible.

It's just the tip of the iceberg. Most organizations, if tracking cost of quality at all, track the obvious – like these listed below:

- Scrap, rework, repair, rejects
- Warranty, recalls, customer returns
- Inspection and testing costs

Your organization's list may vary. Yet while the costs listed above are important and must be tracked and addressed, there are many more

Section 3: Practices and Methodologies

costs of quality to consider. Cost of quality is typically measured in four categories, as described below, with a few examples to consider for each category. Please note that this is not an exhaustive list; it is a sample intended to help you start to examine where you may focus your efforts.

1. **Appraisal Costs** are activities associated with assuring a product or service conforms to performance requirements and standards
2. **Prevention Costs** are activities intended to prevent poor quality in products or services
3. **Internal Failure Costs** are activities associated with a product or service not meeting standards or customer requirements prior to delivery to the customer
4. **External Failure Costs** are activities associated with a product or service not meeting standards or customer requirements at delivery or after delivery to the customer

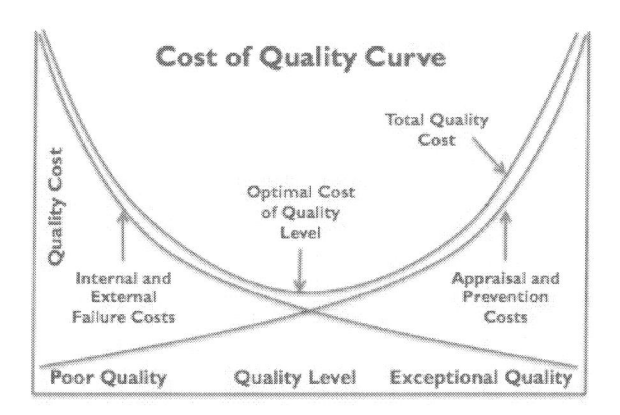

Cost of Quality Curve

Total Quality Cost

Optimal Cost of Quality Level

Internal and External Failure Costs

Appraisal and Prevention Costs

Quality Cost | Poor Quality — Quality Level — Exceptional Quality

In the examples listed on the next page, you will notice that not all quality costs are bad. The goal is to balance the good quality costs of appraisal and prevention with the wasteful quality costs of internal and external failures, while reducing your overall quality costs. Typically, as you work to decrease internal and external failure costs, you will begin to spend more on appraisal and prevention.

Section 3: Practices and Methodologies

Appraisal Costs	Prevention Costs
• Inspections, Evaluations, Tests, and Review of Data • Laboratory Support and Equipment • Qualification of Supplier Product and Purchasing Appraisal • Product or Service Quality Audits • Measurement Equipment, Maintenance, and Calibration • Outside Certifications	• Process Planning • Training and Education • Process Controls, Validations, and Audits • Quality Function Expenses • Performance Reporting • Marketing Research and Customer Surveys
Internal Failure Costs	**External Failure Costs**
• Failure to Scale Up • Poor Communication and Documentation • Uncontrolled Material Losses • Material Review, Disposition, and Corrective Action • Rework, Repair, Retest, Reinspection, and Investigation Support • Supplier Failure, Reject, and Replacement	• Surgical Error or Incorrect Prescription • Customer Goodwill • Retrofit Costs and Warranty Claims • Recall Costs and Returned Goods • Liability Costs and Penalties • Customer Compliant Investigation

Carefully selecting your initiatives and projects will allow you to focus on costs that prevent direct negative impact to your customers. I believe it is paramount that you set your goal to execute initiatives that move the majority of your quality costs into the category of prevention, and reduce or eliminate your external failure quality costs – where your customer is directly and negatively impacted.

Organizations operating at optimal quality levels may spend less than five percent of their revenues fixing problems, while those operating at average quality levels may spend up to 30 percent of their revenues fixing problems.

Wishing you much success in your pursuit of understanding and managing your quality costs, thereby generating greater value in your organization!

Section 3: Practices and Methodologies

A3 PDCA, LSS DMAIC, and DfLSS DMADV

You wouldn't use a hammer to put a screw in the wall, or a screwdriver to put a nail in a board, would you? The same can be said for selecting a problem-solving or continuous-improvement methodology. Don't be a "MacGyver" when selecting a methodology to employ for your organizational initiative. Make the best choice by aligning the methodology's tools and strengths. Doing so will effectively and efficiently achieve greater success – aligning the type of effort, goals, and deliverables – for your initiative.

Some methodologies are backward looking, meaning that the methodologies are suited for issues or problems that currently exist. And other methodologies are forward looking – better suited for developing and defining something entirely new. Regardless of the methodology you choose, undoubtedly you will include solid project management techniques and practices to complement and support project phases and execution. None of the methodologies will be successful without applying foundational project management practices, which are frequently left out of the continuous improvement project lifecycle, and often result in schedule delays, scope creep, missed steps, and budget misses.

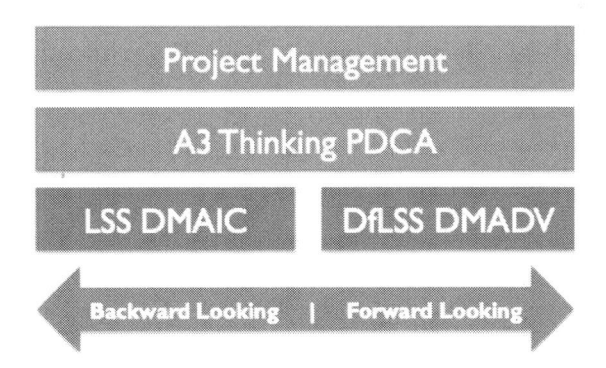

```
┌─────────────────────────────────┐
│      Project Management         │
├─────────────────────────────────┤
│       A3 Thinking PDCA          │
├──────────────┬──────────────────┤
│  LSS DMAIC   │   DfLSS DMADV    │
└──────────────┴──────────────────┘
  ← Backward Looking | Forward Looking →
```

There are many methodologies that could be included in this chapter (8D, Shainin®, Kepner-Tregoe®, to list a few), yet this chapter is focused on the problem-solving and continuous-improvement methodologies of A3 Thinking PDCA, Lean Six Sigma (LSS) DMAIC, and Design for Lean Six Sigma (DfLSS) DMADV.

Section 3: Practices and Methodologies

Next is a simple matrix depicting how phases align across these three methodologies. Following the matrix is a short description of each methodology and its phases, as well as an image of a decision diagram that may be used to help determine when you will most likely choose a specific methodology.

A3 Thinking PDCA	LSS DMAIC	DfLSS DMADV
Plan	Define	Define
	Measure	Measure
	Analyze	Analyze
Do	Improve	Design
Check/Act	Control	Verify

A3 Thinking PDCA (also known as **PDSA**) is a forward- or backward-looking methodology and may be used as a continuous-improvement cycle, for root cause problem-solving, as an approach to design a new product, service, or process, or as a method to implement change.

- **Plan** – Define goals, determine causes and requirements, and develop the A3 plan
- **Do** – Implement the plan by launching new or improved product, process, or service
- **Check/Study** – Measure and study the actual results against planned results for potential actions
- **Act** – Conduct training, implement corrective action, begin continuous improvement, and adjust based on results of check/study phase

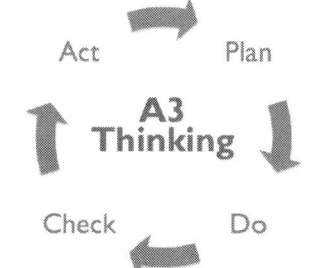

Lean Six Sigma (LSS) DMAIC is a backward-looking methodology employed when a product, service, or process is not currently meeting customer requirements. DMAIC is typically heavy on data collection and statistical analysis, and is used on a wide variety of quality-improvement and problem-solving opportunities.

- **Define** the problem and goal, and develop a project charter

Section 3: Practices and Methodologies

- **Measure** the problem and current-state process by collecting relevant and fact-based data
- **Analyze** the data and determine root cause of the problem
- **Improve** by implementing solutions to correct and prevent the root cause of the problem
- **Control** inputs necessary to sustain implemented improvements

Design for Lean Six Sigma (DfLSS) DMADV is a forward-looking methodology selected when designing a new – or correcting an existing, irreparably broken – product, service, or process, in order to meet customer requirements. Other variations of DfLSS DMADV include IDOV, IDDOV, and DMADOV.

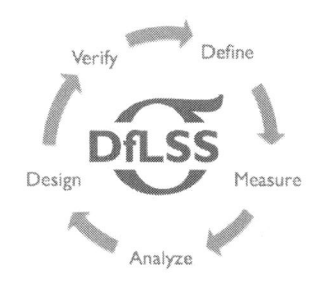

- **Define** the project goal and deliverables, and develop a project charter
- **Measure** to determine customer requirements and expectations
- **Analyze** customer requirements to determine design options
- **Design** and deploy new product, service, or process to meet customer requirements
- **Verify** the product, service, or process output and performance against customer requirements

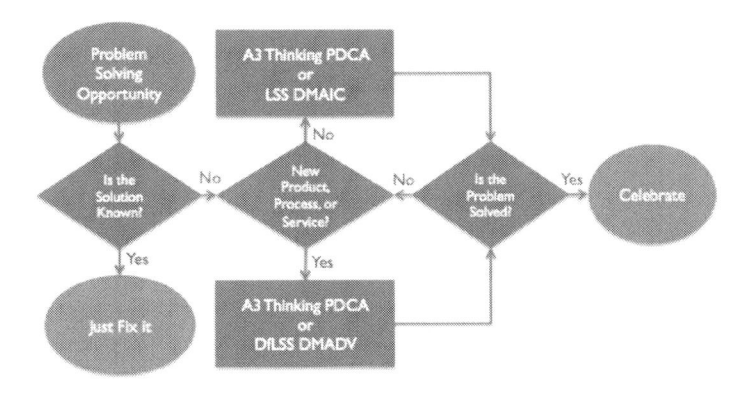

Section 3: Practices and Methodologies

LSS DMAIC and DfLSS DMADV methodologies are often selected over PDCA when the initiative requires significant data collection, analysis, and advanced statistical techniques.

Wishing you much success in your pursuit of operational excellence through methodology selection and execution, thereby generating greater value in your organization!

A3 Thinking

A3 originated with Toyota, due to efforts to get reporting to a concise, one-page, 11"x17" (A3 size) sheet of paper. These days, it includes much more and is known as A3 Thinking or Lean Thinking. Foundationally, A3 Thinking can be thought of as being supported by problems solving, mentoring and coaching, communication, and collaboration. There are seven key elements to A3 Thinking.

Seven Elements of A3 Thinking:

- **Logical Thinking Process** – using scientific method and PDCA (Plan, Do, Check, Act) to get to the root cause
- **Objectivity** – use of facts and data to define the problem
- **Results and Process** – balancing between methodology and achieving results
- **Synthesis, Visualization, Distillation** – concise visual display of the information and data
- **Alignment** – having consensus of the problem causes and countermeasures
- **Coherency Within and Consistency Across** – results in a linkage to the root cause, countermeasures, company goals, and departmental/functional goals
- **Systems Viewpoint** – impact of countermeasures

The problem-solving methodology used in A3 Thinking is based on the continuous improvement cycle known as the Deming Cycle or PDCA. While the Deming Cycle from the 1950's included actions and activities conducted in each of the four phases, I would like to apply the phases in alignment to the flow through described in the following image of an A3 Report.

Section 3: Practices and Methodologies

A3 Report Layout with PDCA

Background - Why work on the Problem - When and Where did the Problem Start	**Future State and Countermeasures** - Depict the Future Process - Who, What, and When
Current State - Define the Problem - Depict the Current Process	
Goals and Objectives - What Constitutes Success - When will it be Completed	**Check Results and Impacts** - Measures and Metrics - Control Charts or Scorecard
Root Cause Analysis - Cause and Effect Diagram - 5 Why and Graphical Diagrams	**Follow-up** - Conduct Training - Adjust as Required

The A3 Report resides on an 11"x17" sheet of paper; it may be used for various purposes, including problem solving, proposals, design efforts, and more. However, it typically is built in the layout above. While the A3 report of the past has been a living document using paper and pencil, many A3 reports today take the form of an Excel or PowerPoint template. The keys are the A3 Thinking and the PDCA methodology. By putting A3 Thinking together with PDCA and the A3 Report, you now have a powerful problem-solving approach, which can be used at all levels of the organization to solve problems, and to report on the status and progress.

Benefits of A3 Thinking include:

- Consistent approach with common language
- Improved problem solving, decision making, and reduced risks
- Improved customer satisfaction with quality results
- Faster cycle times with less waste at a reduced cost
- Improved speed and sustainment of problem resolution
- Improved culture, employee engagement, and problem solving

Utilizing this consistent, powerful, and proven approach results in strengthening the capabilities of the workforce, accelerating the speed to resolution of problem solving, and the generation of valuable results.

Wishing you much success in your pursuit of A3 "Lean" Thinking, thereby generating greater value in your organization!

Section 3: Practices and Methodologies

Lean Six Sigma (LSS) DMAIC

Lean Six Sigma – the mythical, magical, and sometimes even scary and threatening topic – yet, is it really as complicated as it might seem at first glance? While a discussion about Lean Six Sigma could take many forms – including that of a strategy, a business process, a toolkit, a quality level, and a methodology, this chapter will be focused on Lean Six Sigma DMAIC as an improvement and problem-solving methodology.

I would like to submit that **DMAIC** is not mythical, magical, or even complicated, for that matter. When broken down into its five phases (**D**efine – **M**easure – **A**nalyze – **I**mprove – **C**ontrol), it actually becomes quite simple and even approaches the notion of common sense. In it's simplest form, the phases take on the following characteristics and outcomes:

- **Define** the problem and goal, and develop a project charter
- **Measure** the problem and current state by collecting relevant and fact-based data
- **Analyze** the data and determine root cause of the problem
- **Improve** by implementing solutions to correct and prevent the root cause
- **Control** the inputs necessary to sustain implemented improvements

I realize the explanation above is a bit of an over simplification of the Lean Six Sigma DMAIC methodology. Yet, when you boil it down, wouldn't you want to approach improvement projects or problems in this way? While the description is the common-sense version, let's add more tools and detail to DMAIC's phases, thereby providing necessary information to achieve outcomes.

Section 3: Practices and Methodologies

Define Phase Tools and Approaches	Define Phase Deliverables
• Project charter/project contract • Requirements gathering • Stakeholder analysis • Work breakdown structure (WBS) • SIPOC and flowcharting	• Define problem statement, SMART goal, and scope • Define customers and Critical-to-Quality (CTQ) • Identify sponsor, coach, lead, and team • Define high-level project plan • Define high-level process flow

Measure Phase Tools and Approaches	Measure Phase Deliverables
• Input/output or swimlane process mapping • Cause-and-Effect diagram and X-Y Matrix • Data collection plan and sample sizes • Measurement Systems Analysis (MSA) • Capability Studies	• Validate SIPOC and detailed process maps • Identify Cause-and-Effect relationships • Collect data for analysis and baseline metrics • Validate measurement system • Determine process capability

Analyze Phase Tools and Approaches	Analyze Phase Deliverables

• Hypothesis testing, correlation, regression
• Cause-and-Effect and "5 Whys"
• Graphical Analysis, Pareto, scatter plot, etc.
• Prioritization matrix
• Swimlane or value-stream analysis
• Financial and operational analysis
	• Identify the root causes
	   ○ Source of the defects, issues, or variation
	   ○ Critical few inputs resulting in the output
	• Prioritize root causes
	• Identify non-value-added activities
	• Define achievable benefits

Improve Phase Tools and Approaches	Improve Phase Deliverables
• Design of Experiments (DOE) • Brainstorming and Affinity diagrams • Solution Selection matrix or Pugh matrix • Failure Modes and Effects Analysis (FMEA) • Work breakdown and project plan	• Optimize process settings • List of potential solutions • Prioritize solutions • Determine potential failures of solutions • Pilot solutions and define implementation plan

Section 3: Practices and Methodologies

Control Phase Tools and Approaches	Control Phase Deliverables
• Financial and operational analysis	• Validate improvements and benefits
• Control plan and SPC	• Validate sustained improvement
• Work breakdown and project plan	• Close and hand-off to process owner
• Team celebration	• Celebrate!

Lean Six Sigma DMAIC, as opposed to other methodologies, is heavily weighted in statistical analysis. Therefore, the Analyze phase may be a bit daunting for the non-statistician; however, it is manageable with support from a Lean Six Sigma coach or mentor.

Lean Six Sigma is a standardized approach to problem solving and continuous improvement, with the goal of improving quality, speed, and cost of processes, services, and products. Jack Welch said, "Six Sigma is the most important initiative GE has ever undertaken...it is part of the genetic code of our future leadership."

Benefits of Lean Six Sigma include:

- Consistent approach with a common language
- Improved problem solving, decision making, and reduced risks
- Improved customer satisfaction with quality results
- Faster cycle times with less waste at a reduced cost
- Reduced variation and improved quality
- Improved speed and sustainment of problem resolution
- Improved culture, employee engagement, and continuous improvement

Since Motorola's CEO Bob Galvin, along with Bill Smith and Mikel Harry, introduced the early form of Six Sigma DMAIC in the late 1980s, it has been proven successful over and over again, by companies in every industry. Still, many companies struggle with the adoption of the rigor necessary to successfully execute DMAIC. When followed, the discipline of Lean Six Sigma DMAIC may be applied to nearly any size problem or improvement project in any industry, with amazing results.

Wishing you much success in your pursuit of continuous improvement and problem solving through the rigor and discipline of Lean Six Sigma DMAIC, thereby generating greater value in your organization!

Section 3: Practices and Methodologies

Design for Lean Six Sigma (DfLSS) DMADV

Design for Lean Six Sigma DMADV is a very powerful methodology and tool set for developing and deploying a new and defect-free product, process, or service. Based on the concept of Lean Six Sigma DMAIC, Design for Lean Six Sigma DMADV is a forward-looking methodology ideally employed when designing new – or correcting an existing, irreparably broken – product, service, or process in order to meet customer requirements. Other variations of DMADV include IDOV, IDDOV, and DMADOV.

Design for Lean Six Sigma DMADV utilizes a front-loaded approach to the development process, which in turn results in lesser overall cost, faster launch, and fewer after-launch issues. As seen in the development curve image, DfLSS starts applying resources early in the development timeline and those resources taper off quickly after launch. Comparatively, the traditional approach ramps up the resource allocation through launch, with peak use of resources after launch. Note: DfLSS becomes especially powerful when aligned and employed with the rigor of a defined new product development (NPD) process.

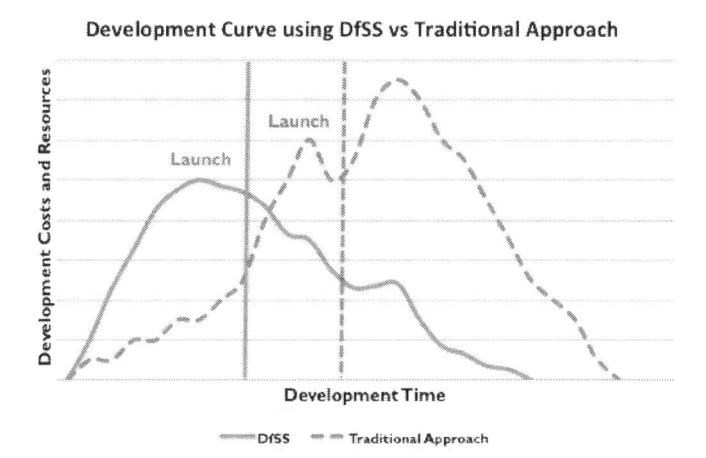

Development Curve using DfSS vs Traditional Approach

Section 3: Practices and Methodologies

DMADV, broken down (**D**efine, **M**easure, **A**nalyze, **D**esign, **V**erify) and in its simplest form, takes on the following characteristics and outcomes:

- **Define** the project goal and deliverables, and develop a project charter
- **Measure** to determine customer requirements and expectations
- **Analyze** customer requirements to determine design options
- **Design** and deploy new product, process, or service to meet customer requirements
- **Verify** the product, process, or service output and performance against customer requirements

Benefits of Design for Lean Six Sigma include:

- Consistent approach with a common language
- Improved decision making with reduced risks
- Improved designs of new products, processes, and services
- Improved customer satisfaction with quality results
- Improved development times at a reduced cost
- Improved culture, employee engagement, and continuous improvement

Let's include more tools and detail – in the following table – to the simple version of DMADV's phases, thereby providing additional information to achieve outcomes.

Define Phase Tools and Approaches	Define Phase Deliverables
• Project charter/project contract • Stakeholder analysis • Work breakdown structure (WBS) • SIPOC	• Project description, SMART goal, and scope • Sponsor, coach, lead, and team launched • High-level project plan defined • High-level depiction of as-is condition

Section 3: Practices and Methodologies

Measure Phase Tools and Approaches	Measure Phase Deliverables

• Data collection plan and sample sizes
• Measurement Systems Analysis (MSA)
• Input/output process maps
• Requirements gathering
• Voice of Customer (VOC) and Voice of Business (VOB)
  • Affinity Diagram and KJ Analysis
  • Kano Model
	• Collect data for analysis and baseline metrics
	• Validate measurement system
	• Validate SIPOC and critical process characteristics
	• Customers defined and prioritized
	• VOC and VOB translated into Critical-to-Quality (CTQ)
	• CTQs categorized and prioritized
	• Satisfiers and exciters identified

Analyze Phase Tools and Approaches	Analyze Phase Deliverables
• Quality Function Deployment 1 (QFD)/House of Quality (HOQ) • Performance Scorecard • Financial and operational analysis	• CTQ/CTC engineering characteristics identified and prioritized • Performance characteristics defined for scoring • Define achievable benefits

Design Phase Tools and Approaches	Design Phase Deliverables
• TRIZ • Pugh Matrix • Design for X (DFX) • Transfer Functions • DFMEA • Design Validation Plan • QFD House 2 • Product Scorecard • QFD/HOQ 3 • 3P (Lean VSM) • PFMEA • Process Scorecard	• Concept generation • Concept selection • Design for all phases of the lifecycle • Design for simplicity • Design failure modes analyzed • Design validation • CTQ/CTC part characteristics prioritized • Characteristics scored for capability • CTQ/CTC process operations prioritized • Product and Process Preparation • Process failure modes analyzed • Process scored for capability

Section 3: Practices and Methodologies

Verify Phase Tools and Approaches	Verify Phase Deliverables
• QFD/HOQ 4 • Performance Scorecard • Summary Scorecard • Financial and operational analysis • Control plan and SPC • Work breakdown and project plan • Team celebration	• CTQ/CTC production requirements prioritized • Performance characteristics scored for capability • Scorecard rollup • Validation of improvements and benefits • Validation of sustained improvement • Project closed and hand-off • Celebrate!

You may choose to utilize the full toolset and power of DMADV to develop and deploy a complex product or service. However, you might, for example, decide to use a much smaller subset of the DfLSS tools to develop and deploy a simple process. When followed, the discipline of DfLSS DMADV may be applied to nearly any size development and deployment project in any industry, with astonishing results.

Wishing you much success in your pursuit of developing and deploying defect-free products, processes, and services through the application of Design for Lean Six Sigma DMADV, thereby generating greater value in your organization!

Theory of Constraints (TOC)

What if your customers want more of your product than you can produce, and they want it now? While this is a great opportunity for your organization, what would you do? Might you add another shift, install another line, or expand to another building? Or, do you determine how to get more product through the bottleneck of your existing processes? If you could figure out how to get more product volume through your existing processes, you would generate additional revenue more quickly, resulting in increased profit for your business. To find a solution, you might wish to apply Theory of Constraints (TOC). It is a simple, yet effective, approach to improve a process's throughput, and to include in your toolbox.

Section 3: Practices and Methodologies

Eliyahu M. Goldratt introduced Theory of Constraints in his 1984 book, The Goal. It is based on the idea that the throughput of a process, value stream, or system is limited only by its constraints or bottlenecks. The methodology is used to identify – and improve or eliminate – the constraint, which restricts or prevents a process from achieving its throughput goal. Martin Villeneuve, Canadian screenwriter, film producer, and director, said, "Problems are hidden opportunities, and constraints can actually boost creativity."

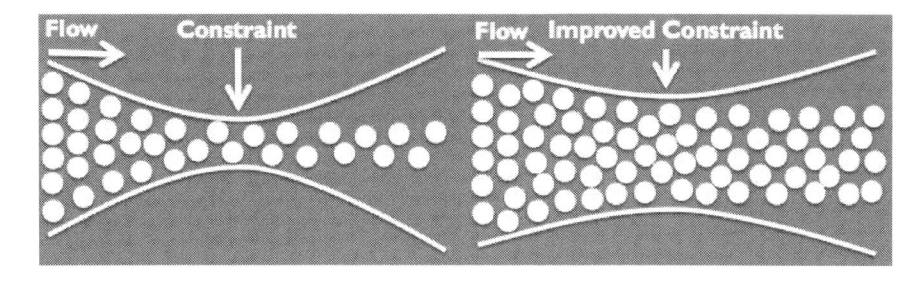

Benefits of Theory of Constraints include:

- Improved process throughput of a product or service
- Increased profitability through achieving a throughput goal
- Increased productivity, capacity, and quality
- Reduced lead times and inventory levels
- Improved customer satisfaction
- Improved culture, employee engagement, and problem solving

Theory of Constraints Cycle:

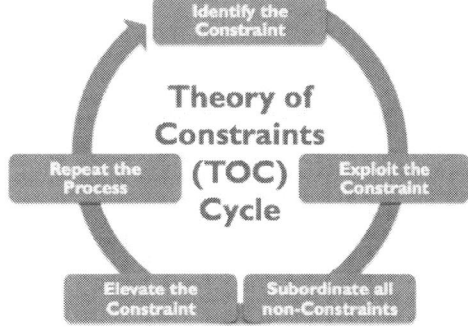

1. **Evaluate** current-state process and identify constraint that limits achieving throughput goal
2. **Exploit** constraint by making small and rapid improvements to the process at constraint location
3. **Subordinate** all other steps and activities in the process to focus on the constraint, ensuring they support improvements to the constraint

Section 3: Practices and Methodologies

4. **Elevate** constraint in the process to successfully achieve throughput goal by applying more advanced and sustainable improvements; this step is considered as "breaking" the constraint, and may result in identifying a constraint somewhere else in the process
5. **Repeat** the continuous improvement cycle for additional or new constraints that limit or prevent the process from achieving throughput goal

Tools and inputs that may be used in the Theory of Constraints cycle include Pareto analysis, flow charts, process maps, scorecards, RACI matrix, SIPOC diagram, 5 Why root-cause analysis, cause-and-effect diagram, affinity diagram, brainstorming, multivoting, and nominal group technique.

Constraints may be internal to your processes, systems, and organization, such as policies, people, and equipment. USA President Ronald Reagan once said, "There are no constraints on the human mind, no walls around the human spirit, no barriers to our progress, except those we ourselves erect." Constraints may also be external to your organization, such as changing regulations or resource scarcity.

Regardless of internal or external constraint types, applying Theory of Constraints is an excellent approach to identifying, improving, or eliminating the constraint. Theory of Constraints is a continuous improvement cycle, which can be used as a stand-alone methodology to improve throughput, or as a supporting methodology to A3 Thinking, Lean Six Sigma, or Design for Lean Six Sigma.

Wishing you much success in your pursuit of achieving throughput goals through constraint management, thereby generating greater value in your organization!

Section 4: Project Management

Another key element of the operational excellence transformation is disciplined and structured project management. This section of the handbook includes chapters representing tools and plans related specifically to processes, methodology, and rigor applicable to the discipline of project management.

- Project Lifecycle Management
  - Project Toolbox
    - Business Case Proposal
    - Charter
    - Requirements Document
    - Financial Reporting
    - Stakeholder Management Plan
    - Work Breakdown Structure
    - Resource Plan
    - Contact List
    - Schedule and Gantt Chart
    - Communication Plan
      - Informative Communication
      - Concise Communication
    - Quality Management Plan
    - Procurement Management Plan
    - Risk Management Plan
    - Issue Management Plan
    - Change Control Plan
    - Lessons-Learned Plan
    - Checklist
    - Close-out and Sign-off

Please consider these as essential ingredients to successful project management and the value generation journey.

Section 4: Project Management

Project Lifecycle Management

Managing the project lifecycle consists of applying processes, methodology, and rigor to achieve specific deliverables and goals, as defined in the project charter and project plan. It includes managing resources and applying the knowledge and skills necessary to achieve goals and deliverables within defined scope, schedule, and budget. Project management typically consists of managing a cross-functional, diverse project team – one in which members do not normally work together or have the same background and skill set.

Projects are constrained by scope, schedule, and budget; typically, they are launched to deliver a product, service, or improvement by adding value for the organization and customer. A project has a defined beginning and end, and is considered temporary in nature. A project is different from daily or routine operations, which consist of repetitive functions or activities.

What better way to manage a project lifecycle and its team than to use PMI®'s PMBOK® 5th Edition processes? The forty-seven processes are arranged in five process groups and ten knowledge areas, as defined in the following table.

Knowledge Areas	Initiating Process Group	Planning Process Group	Executing Process Group	Monitoring and Controlling Process Group	Closing Process Group
Project Integration Management	Develop Project Charter	Develop Project Management Plan	Direct and Manage Project Work	Monitor and Control Project Work Perform Integrated Change Control	Close Project or Phase
Project Scope Management		Plan Scope Management Collect Requirements Define Scope Create WBS		Validate Scope Control Scope	
Project Time Management		Plan Schedule Management Define Activities Sequence Activities Estimate Activity Resources Estimate Activity Durations Develop Schedule		Control Schedule	
Project Cost Management		Plan Cost Management Estimate Costs Determine Budget		Control Costs	
Project Quality Management		Plan Quality Management	Perform Quality Assurance	Control Quality	

Section 4: Project Management

Project Human Resource Management		Plan Human Resource Management	Acquire Project Team Develop Project Team Manage Project Team		
Project Communication Management		Plan Communication Management	Manage Communications	Control Communications	
Project Risk Management		Plan Risk Management Identify Risks Perform Qualitative Risk Analysis Perform Quantitative Risk Analysis Plan Risk Response		Control Risks	
Project Procurement Management		Plan Procurement Management	Conduct Procurement	Control Procurement	Close Procurement
Project Stakeholder Management	Identify Stakeholders	Plan Stakeholder Management	Manage Stakeholder Engagement	Control Stakeholder Engagement	

Benefits of using processes, methodology, and rigor for project management include:

- Improved quality and customer satisfaction
- Provide a collaborative team environment
- Provide an approach for efficiently and effectively delivering results
- Increase focus and attention on maintaining scope, schedule, and budget
- Save cost and time by applying a methodical, rigorous approach to managing the project
- Provide a consistent approach for delivering the product, process, service, or improvement

Not all projects are created equal – in value or complexity – and not all projects require the same level of rigor in application of processes and methodology. Methods may vary, such as Waterfall, Agile, Lean Project Management, Lean Six Sigma DMAIC, and others. Generally, however, all projects will use and include some level of methodology, rigor, and discipline until project completion or termination. The level of methodology, rigor, and discipline is dependent on the complexity and value of the project. When complexity and value are minimal, apply simple use of the processes and methodology; when complexity and value are at maximum, however, apply full rigor and discipline of the PMI® processes and methodology.

Section 4: Project Management

Regardless of your project value, size, and complexity, you will want to consider these elements of processes, methodology, and rigor as you manage the project lifecycle:

- Create a project toolbox to manage your plans, templates, and artifacts
- Develop a project charter with clear scope, goals, deliverables, and metrics for success
- Understand, manage, and control your stakeholders
- Communicate, communicate, communicate
- Plan, form, develop, and manage your project team and resources
- Develop a project plan, schedule, action plan, and checklist
- Plan, manage, and control scope, schedule, and budget
- Analyze, plan, manage, and control issues, risks, and changes
- Plan, manage, and control quality
- Conduct status reports and updates
- Conduct lessons-learned session, project-close steps, and sign-off process
- Celebrate!

Wishing you much success in your pursuit of project management, thereby generating greater value in your organization!

Project Toolbox

Have you ever found it time consuming and difficult to manage or find all of your project artifacts when using separate documents or different document formats? The suggestion of this chapter is to develop a customized project toolbox – one that contains each of the tools and artifacts your organization typically uses to manage projects.

A project toolbox is helpful when the project requires the use of many project-related tools and templates, and project artifacts will:

- Be accessed during the project lifecycle by many project resources
- Be saved for future use and reference

Section 4: Project Management

- Serve as starting points for future projects

Benefits of a project toolbox include:

- Provide a standardized set of tools and templates for project governance
- Provide a consistent approach for managing project and governance artifacts
- Provide a collaborative team environment
- Provide a common approach to reference and use historical project information
- Save cost and time by combining project artifacts in one toolbox document

Your project toolbox will include all typically used project tools; the project manager and team may choose to use or not use a specific tool, based on the project size and complexity. Each tool in the toolbox is used as a component of the project lifecycle or as a stand-alone tool for use outside of managing a project.

In the context of a project lifecycle, rather than a stand-alone tool, the table below includes a short description of each of the typical tools and artifacts that reside within the project toolbox. In most instances the description and use are the same, yet some of the tools are used for very different reasons when employed outside of the project lifecycle.

The Project Toolbox	
Artifact	Description
Business Case Proposal	Template describing the scope, impact, opportunity, and need for launching a project
Charter	Template that becomes the project contract; contains (at a minimum) the project name and description, problem statement, in/out-of-scope descriptions, success criteria/metrics for success, goals and objectives, team, sponsor, and project manager; may include dependencies, risks, and issues
Requirements Document	Document containing requirements defined by project stakeholders and customers
Financials	Template describing project financial benefits and costs

Section 4: Project Management

Stakeholder Management Plan	Plan that includes stakeholders, their roles, their influence, interest, and support for the project
Work Breakdown Structure	Template that describes the project in three levels – task, sub-task, and work package
Resource Plan	Plan including project roles, team members' names, effort required, start date, and end date
Contact List	Detailed list of project stakeholders, as well as their roles, locations, time zones, telephone numbers, e-mail addresses
Project Schedule	Schedule describing the project in terms of activity name, start date, end date, percent complete, dependencies, and status
Communication Plan	Template detailing project communications relative to audience, timing, delivery channel, dates and times, etc.
Quality Management Plan	Plan describing quality assurance and quality control for the project lifecycle
Procurement Management Plan	Plan describing procurement requirements, responsibilities, and approach for the project lifecycle
Risk Management Plan	Plan describing the project's risks, mitigation actions, and status
Issue Management Plan	Plan describing project issues, along with issue owner, action, and date
Change Control Plan	Plan detailing project scope, schedule, budget changes, and status of change
Lessons-Learned Plan	Plan describing lessons learned and improvement strategies throughout the project lifecycle
Checklist	List of plans, tools, and artifacts required to be completed for a specific project
Close-out/Sign-off	Template used to document the final results and approvals for scope, schedule, and budget
Additional Artifacts from Tools Selection and Use	
Cause-and-Effect Diagram	Graphic template depicting potential causes for the effect being investigated
Cause-and-Effect Matrix	Matrix template describing process inputs or causes, as well as strength of relationships to process outputs or results being investigated
Control Plan	Template used to define a control plan for solution being implemented; includes control characteristics, measurement method, frequency of measurement, who conducts the measurement, signal, and corrective action

Section 4: Project Management

Data Collection Plan	Template detailing data collection plan for the project, including sample size; from whom, when, and where the data will be collected
FMEA	Template used to conduct a Failure Modes and Effect Analysis of chosen solution and to determine mitigations to prevent future issues
Force Field Analysis	Template describing the forces driving for and against the project
Impact/Effort Matrix	Template used to evaluate potential solutions against impact to goal and effort to implement
RACI	Form describing who is **R**esponsible, **A**ccountable, **C**onsulted, and **I**nformed regarding the activities conducted during project lifecycle
Solution-Selection Matrix	Matrix template used to develop and evaluate a list of potential solutions against criteria critical to the project and organizational goals
Status Report	Block chart used for project report-outs that describes the project, activities to take action on before the next report-out, activities conducted since the last report-out, issues, concerns, and resolutions
Training Plan	Plan detailing training to be conducted as a result of the project; includes topic, trainer, audience, date, duration, and delivery method

Your project toolbox may include these listed tools and artifacts, as well as others that you have found especially useful and necessary for your organization's projects. Typically the project toolbox is created in slide-deck or spreadsheet format. Either format seems to work well depending on the organization and its preferences. I prefer creating the project toolbox in a spreadsheet format, with a tab for each tool and artifact. And, I prefer to copy specific templates into PowerPoint slides for presentation.

Once the toolbox template is created and posted in your project documentation library, you will then train your project managers to use it and to communicate it throughout the organization.

Wishing you much success in your pursuit of managing projects with a defined project toolbox, thereby generating greater value in your organization!

Section 4: Project Management

Business Case Proposal

Resources, money, and time are limited, and not every project idea will be launched as an active project. A project business case proposal is a great tool to use to clearly define the proposed project, socialize the idea for input and support, and document the proposed project for official and final go/no go disposition.

A project business case proposal may be used when:

- There are existing customer issues, complaints, and warranty claims
- Project has been identified through a selection and prioritization process
- There has been a project suggestion identified by a business, process, or functional owner
- There is an opportunity to develop and deploy a new and improved product, process, or service
- There is an opportunity to reduce cost, lead-time, non-value-added activities, or quality problems

Benefits of a project business case proposal include:

- Provide a collaborative team environment
- Provide a consistent approach for defining and presenting project proposals
- Increase focus and attention on project clarification, justification, and disposition
- Provide an approach for efficiently and effectively determining disposition of project proposals

Elements of consideration for a project business case proposal:

- **Title Section** – Project business case proposal title, sponsor, project manager, impacted business or function, business owner, and strategy supported
- **Problem/Opportunity** – Problem or business opportunity prompting this proposed project
- **Proposal Input** – Managers and resources who provided input to the proposed project

Section 4: Project Management

- **Benefits** – Financial, technical, quality, or cultural benefits that this proposed project is expected to deliver
- **In-Scope/Out-of-Scope** – In- and out-of-scope elements of this proposed project
- **Risk of Not Doing** – Financial, customer, or compliance risks if the proposed project *is not* initiated
- **Impacts** – Resources, processes, or operations impacted if this proposed project *is* initiated
- **Other** – Information pertinent to the project proposal

Project Business Case Proposal Process:

1. Determine potential project to propose
2. Socialize the potential project with key stakeholders for feedback
3. Define elements of the project business case proposal
4. Secure input on business case proposal elements
5. Document project business case proposal
6. Secure approval to initiate proposed project

Business Case Proposal Process

Potential project → Socialize potential project → Define elements of proposal → Secure input on proposal → Document proposal → Secure approval

An example of a project business case proposal being used is a customer service call center manager who wants to improve customer support by reducing the number of dropped calls and long wait times for customers calling the center. Customers are dropping off the call after dialing in to the call center; the drop rate is one out of four calls. And those calls that did not drop experienced a minimum wait time of sixteen minutes to speak with a service representative. The call center manager defines the proposed project, including the opportunity, benefit, scope, goal, deliverables, and resources required. The manager socializes the proposed project with key stakeholders and develops a business case proposal, which is presented for approval and launch of the customer support improvement project.

While your project business case proposal template may vary slightly, it will likely contain many of the components found in the following

Section 4: Project Management

example. This image depicts a basic project business case proposal template, along with its elements.

Regardless of your project business case proposal template, format, and layout, it is a basis for defining, documenting, and gaining approval and support to launch your proposed project.

Wishing you much success in your pursuit of building a business case for project approval and launch, thereby generating greater value in your organization!

Charter

The project charter is likely the single most important document (or artifact) during the project lifecycle, in the project toolbox. Yet many times it is created, filed, and never reviewed again. Albert Einstein is often credited with the quote, "If I had an hour to solve a problem, I'd spend 55 minutes thinking about the problem and 5 minutes thinking about solutions." While the quote may be found in many forms, the basic premise is always the same: Invest time up front to ensure a successful outcome.

Project charter is the key tool in a project lifecycle in which to invest up-front time. It is essentially a contract between the project lead/manager, sponsor, and team by which to execute the project according to clearly and concisely defined deliverables, goal, scope, and success criteria. I believe it is a living document during the early phases of the project lifecycle, and may be revised as new information and facts are discovered. At a minimum, changes to the charter shall be approved by the project manager, sponsor, and team and, in many cases, recorded in the change log.

Benefits of a well-documented project charter include:

- Providing alignment of the vision and goal to team members
- Securing authority to execute to a plan
- Serving as a reference point to ensure focus on the goal
- Providing a baseline for change control
- Describing what success means for the team
- Detailing the current condition and planned future condition

Project Charter development and maintenance process:

1. Project manager drafts the project charter with input from project sponsor
2. Project manager socializes the drafted project charter with key stakeholders (may include team members) for input and feedback
3. Project manager refines project charter based on feedback
4. Project manager reviews the final draft of the project charter with sponsor and team (and key stakeholders, as appropriate) to secure sign-off

Section 4: Project Management

5. Project manager and project team execute the project, as defined in the project charter
6. Project charter may be revised in the early phases of the project lifecycle, based on input from change control, issue management, and/or risk analysis; all project charter revisions are subject to agreement and sign-off, based on original approval requirements

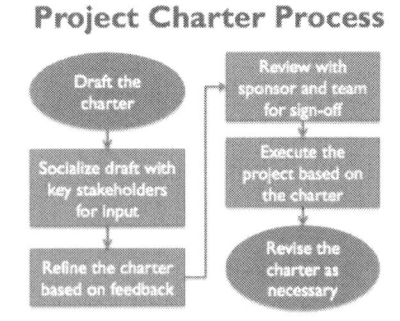

Project Charter Process

- Draft the charter
- Socialize draft with key stakeholders for input
- Refine the charter based on feedback
- Review with sponsor and team for sign-off
- Execute the project based on the charter
- Revise the charter as necessary

Note: You may wish to reference PMBOK® 5th Edition for PMI® processes that make up the knowledge area for project integration management, specifically develop project charter. **Develop project charter** by defining, documenting, and approving the project description, deliverables, goal, scope, and success criteria, thereby providing the project manager authority to apply resources to the project.

Knowledge Areas	Project Management Process Groups				
	Initiating Process Group	Planning Process Group	Executing Process Group	Monitoring and Controlling Process Group	Closing Process Group
Project Integration Management	Develop Project Charter	Develop Project Management Plan	Direct and Manage Project Work	Monitor and Control Project Work Perform Integrated Change Control	Close Project or Phase

Project charter templates may vary based on project types, such as transformation, operational excellence, continuous improvement, Lean Six Sigma, or product/service development and deployment projects. Regardless of the project type, each template will likely contain many of the components found in the following example. This image depicts a basic charter template, along with its elements.

Section 4: Project Management

Project Charter

Project Name:		Charter Date:	Project Number:
Project Sponsor:		Project Manager:	
Impacted Business Department:		Expected Project Cost:	Refined Financial Outcome:

PROJECT DETAIL

PROJECT DESCRIPTION	Problem statement and the benefit statement of the project
PROJECT GOAL	SMART Goal (Specific - Measurable - Achievable - Relevant - Time-bound)
PROJECT SCOPE	In Scope and Out of Scope
SUCCESS CRITERIA	Metrics for Success (Primary and Secondary Metrics)
PROJECT CONCERNS	Issues, Risks, and Dependencies

CHARTER APPROVALS	Approval Date:	Approved by:

PROJECT SPONSOR — The person who sponsors the project, ensuring that resources are available, roadblocks are removed, and cross-functional issues are resolved.
PROJECT MANAGER — The person who leads the project team; develops and executes the project plan; and employs rigor, processes, and methodology.
PROJECT TEAM — Those who bring relevant expertise from the business unit or organization to a particular project and carry out the work of the project.

I believe it is imperative to train and coach your project managers to spend appropriate time developing and socializing the project charter to gain support of the project and sign-offs, as defined.

Wishing you much success in your pursuit of successful project chartering and execution, thereby generating greater value in your organization!

Requirements Document

Critical to the success of any project is gathering, understanding, and managing its requirements. The work of gathering requirements starts pre-launch of the project and may continue being collected and clarified through the planning phase of the project lifecycle. Requirements may be used as input to develop a proposal, quote, statement

Section 4: Project Management

of work (SOW), contract, project plan, project schedule, etc. Based on the project phase and type of project management method employed, and if requirements change, it may be necessary to utilize a change control process. Software engineer leader Steve McConnell is quoted as saying, "The most difficult part of requirements gathering is not the act of recording what the user wants; it is the exploratory development activity of helping users figure out what they want."

A project requirements plan may be used when:

- Project plan and schedule are being developed
- Project is in the beginning phase of the lifecycle
- Proposal or quote is being developed
- Project is intended to deliver a process, product, or service
- Contract or statement of work is being developed for delivery of product or services

Benefits of creating a project requirements plan include:

- Provide a collaborative team environment
- Increase focus and attention on project requirements
- Provide an approach for stakeholder engagement and management
- Provide an approach for efficiently and effectively managing project requirements
- Save cost and time by identifying, categorizing, and managing project requirements
- Provide a consistent approach for identifying, categorizing, and managing project requirements

Requirements typically represent the following *types*:

- **Business** requirements are those intended to support achievement of business goals or strategies through the execution of the project
- **Customer** requirements are provided by and specific to the customer of the project deliverables
- **Functional** requirements are specific to the functionality of the process, product, or service represented by the project
- **Market** requirements are included to achieve specific market needs through the execution of the project

Section 4: Project Management

- **Process** requirements are specific to the process design represented by the project
- **Product** requirements are specific to the product features and characteristics represented by the project
- **Project** requirements are constraints to the project such as scope, schedule, and budget
- **Service** requirements are specific to the service features and characteristics represented by the project
- **Technical** requirements are design requirements for the process, product, or service represented by the project
- **User** requirements are specific to the needs of the user of the process, product, or service represented by the project

Requirements typically fit into one of two *categories*:

- **Must-Have** – requirements designated by the stakeholder as compulsory to the success of the project
- **Nice-to-Have** – requirements identified by the stakeholder as wanted and significant, but optional and not required as a measure of success for the project

Project Requirements Plan Process:

1. Identify need for requirements gathering and planning
2. Initiate requirements plan template
3. Gather and document requirements by consulting stakeholders
4. Define requirements by type and category
5. Assign ownership of requirements, if further action is needed
6. Take necessary action and determine status (to include or not include)

Requirements Plan Process

Identify need → Define type and category
↓ ↓
Initiate plan → Assign ownership
↓ ↓
Gather requirements → Determine status

Note: You may wish to reference PMBOK® 5th Edition for PMI® processes that make up the knowledge area for project scope management, specifically collecting requirements. **Collect requirements** by defining, detailing, and managing stakeholders' needs and requirements necessary to meet project objectives and deliverables.

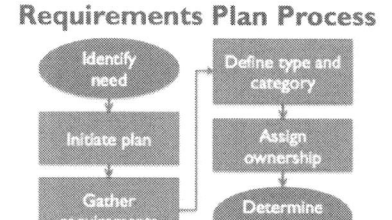

Section 4: Project Management

Knowledge Areas	Project Management Process Groups				
	Initiating Process Group	Planning Process Group	Executing Process Group	Monitoring and Controlling Process Group	Closing Process Group
Project Scope Management		Plan Scope Management Collect Requirements Define Scope Create WBS		Validate Scope Control Scope	

Project requirements may be used as inputs to the project plan, project schedule, action plan, and risk management plan. While your project requirements plan template may vary slightly, it will likely contain many of the components found in the following example. This image depicts a basic project requirements plan template, along with its elements.

Project Requirements Plan								
Project Name:					Project Manager:		Date:	
Who	When	What			Who	What	When	Other
Stakeholder	Date	Requirement	Type	Category	Owner	Action	Status	Date	Comments

Regardless of your project requirements plan template, format, and layout, it is fundamental for larger and more complex projects to include such a document in the project toolbox to support defining the project plan and schedule.

Wishing you much success in your pursuit of effectively gathering project requirements, thereby generating greater value in your organization!

Financial Reporting

Alexa Von Tobel, founder and CEO of LearnVest.com, said, "A good financial plan is a road map that shows us exactly how the choices we make today will affect our future." Conducting project financial reporting in a standardized and consistent format is key to justifying the

Section 4: Project Management

project, gaining support and commitment, and celebrating project success. Planned and realized cash or cost benefits should be projected and reported to enlist support at project initiation, and to ensure recognition when benefits are achieved. Planned cost and realized capital expenses are necessary to execute a project; they should be projected and reported to secure funds when needed and to record expenditures when realized.

Conduct project financial reporting when the project:

- Is expected to realize cost savings or cash flow benefits
- Will require cost or capital expense to execute

Benefits of conducting project financial reporting include:

- Increase focus and attention on project's financial impact
- Ensure recognition is provided for cost savings or cash flow benefits
- Ensure support is provided when expenditures are required
- Provide a consistent approach for reporting project financials
- Provide an approach for efficiently and effectively reporting project financials

An example of using project financial reporting is by a project team formed to reduce defects found on eyeglass polycarbonate lens material at final inspection or by the customer. The team determines that the solution requires a modification to the manufacturing process, as well as adding an in-process optical testing device. Required expenditure to implement the solution is projected to be $12,000, while the cost savings benefit is projected to save $300,000 over a twelve-month period. The team uses a project financial reporting approach to gain support and necessary approvals required to implement the solution, and to report and claim the cost savings benefit over the twelve-month period.

Project Financial Reporting Process:

1. Determine cash or cost benefits to be realized from executing the project
2. Determine costs or capital expenses necessary to execute the project

Section 4: Project Management

3. Originate the "Project Financial Report" template
   a. Inputs to a financial report may include the project charter, requirements document, work breakdown structure, project schedule, and action plan
4. Conduct an initial project financial report call or meeting to gain project support and commitment
5. Conduct regular financial reporting by updating benefits realized or expenses incurred
6. Close financial reporting when the finance representative agrees to declared benefits, incurred expenses, and when the project is closed and signed-off
7. Celebrate realized benefits that resulted by executing the project

Project Financial Reporting Process

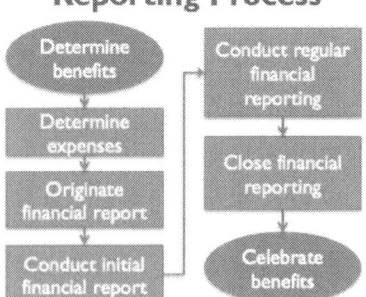

Determine benefits → Determine expenses → Originate financial report → Conduct initial financial report → Conduct regular financial reporting → Close financial reporting → Celebrate benefits

Note: You may wish to reference PMBOK® 5th Edition for PMI® processes that make up the knowledge area for project cost management:

- **Plan cost management** by establishing documentation for planning, managing, disbursing, and controlling costs
- **Estimate costs** by developing an estimate of the monetary resources needed to complete the project
- **Determine budget** by totaling the estimated costs of project activities
- **Control costs** by monitoring, updating, and managing the status of project costs

Knowledge Areas	Project Management Process Groups					
	Initiating Process Group	Planning Process Group	Executing Process Group	Monitoring and Controlling Process Group	Closing Process Group
Project Cost Management		Plan Cost Management, Estimate Costs, Determine Budget		Control Costs	

While your project financial report template may vary slightly, it will likely contain many of the components found in the following example. This image depicts a basic project financial report template, along with its elements.

82

Section 4: Project Management

Project Financial Report								
Project Name:								
Project Manager:		Date:						
Projected(P)/Actual(A) Benefits				Months/Quarters/Years				
	1P	1A	2P	2A	3P	3A	4P	4A
Cash: Improved Cashflow through Inventory Management								
Cash: Improved Cashflow through Receivables Management								
Cost: Expense Reduction from Labor Cost (Salary & Benefits)								
Cost: Expense Reduction from Reduced Hardware & Software Costs								
Cost: Expense Reduction from Reduced Maintenance Fees								
Cost: Expense Reduction from Reduced Operating Cost								
Cost: Expense Reduction from Reduced Unit Cost								
Growth: Increased Revenue from New Sales								
[Additional Benefits]								
[Additional Benefits]								
Total Projected/Actual Benefits	$0	$0	$0	$0	$0	$0	$0	$0
Projected(P)/Actual(A) Costs				Months/Quarters/Years				
	1P	1A	2P	2A	3P	3A	4P	4A
Internal Labor								
Hardware								
Software								
Maintenance								
Travel								
[Additional Costs]								
[Additional Costs]								
Total Projected/Actual Costs	$0	$0	$0	$0	$0	$0	$0	$0
Describe assumptions used when projecting the financial costs or benefits:								

Regardless of your project financial report template, format, and layout, it is fundamental for any project with financial benefits or costs to include such a report in the project toolbox and to review it during project review meetings.

Wishing you much success in your pursuit of projecting and reporting project financials, thereby generating greater value in your organization!

Stakeholder Management Plan

A stakeholder management plan is a significant, success-ensuring artifact to include in your project toolbox and to use during the lifecycle of complex projects. Cameron Sinclair said, "A true architect is

Section 4: Project Management

not an artist, but an optimistic realist. He takes a diverse number of stakeholders; extracts needs, concerns, and dreams; then creates a beautiful – yet tangible – solution that is loved by the users and the community at large." Understanding stakeholders and having a well-executed stakeholder management plan are essential to the success of every project. While a stakeholder management plan is great for the effective and efficient execution of a project, it is very useful for other endeavors in business and may be considered to use in many undertakings.

There are many potential stakeholders for a project, such as anyone or any group who may positively or negatively impact the project lifecycle or outcome. A stakeholder is one who may effect, or one who is affected by, the outcome or change. Stakeholders can be internal or external to the organization, having different needs and different levels of involvement. It is important to identify stakeholders and to discern categories to which they belong.

Categories of stakeholders include:

- Primary stakeholders – those who are directly impacted by the project
- Secondary stakeholders – those who are indirectly impacted by the project
- Key stakeholders – may be primary or secondary, and are those who have significant influence and/or interest in the project

Questions to consider when identifying stakeholders:

- To which stakeholder category do they belong? (Primary, Secondary, Key Stakeholder)
- What is their interest and influence level? (High/Low)
- What is their support level? (Support, Neutral, Against)
- What do they need from us?
- How do they want to receive information and communications?

Stakeholder management is beneficial when:

- There are varying levels of interest, involvement, and support
- Project results in a new process, product, or service
- Project impacts safety, quality, or customer service

Section 4: Project Management

- Project is sensitive or political in nature

Benefits of a stakeholder management plan include:

- Consistent approach for analyzing and defining a strategy for stakeholders
- Consistent approach for communicating with stakeholders
- Address and manage stakeholder needs
- Facilitate securing support for the project
- Provide a collaborative team environment
- Lead to efficient and effective data analysis

Conducting a stakeholder analysis will allow you to use input from the stakeholders to help define the project plan and secure support for the project. The analysis process will enhance stakeholders' understanding of the project, help them understand their role, and learn how they may benefit, as well as provide input and resources, when necessary.

Below is a defined stakeholder management process:

1. Identify stakeholders
2. Their roles, influence level, interest level, and support level are determined and documented on the stakeholder management plan
3. Appropriate strategies are determined, based on the stakeholder evaluation
    a. Low interest/low influence stakeholders: **Monitor** for changing needs and interests
    b. High interest/low influence stakeholders: **Inform** with appropriate levels of communication to safeguard against issues
    c. Low interest/high influence stakeholders: **Satisfy** with levels of communication necessary to meet their needs
    d. High interest/high influence stakeholders: **Manage** by fully engaging them in the process

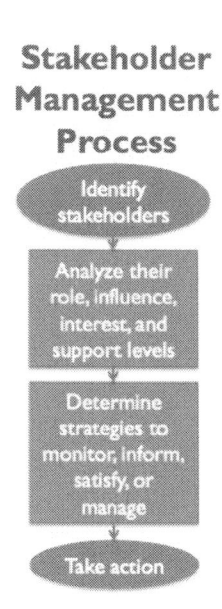

Stakeholder Management Process

- Identify stakeholders
- Analyze their role, influence, interest, and support levels
- Determine strategies to monitor, inform, satisfy, or manage
- Take action

Section 4: Project Management

4. The strategy owner takes action based on the strategy
5. Stakeholders and conditions are reviewed; the process is repeated, if changes occur

Note: You may wish to reference PMBOK® 5th Edition for PMI® processes that make up the knowledge area for project stakeholder management:

- **Identify stakeholders** by recognizing people and groups who could impact or be impacted by the outcome of the project and by determining their influence, interest, and support
- **Plan stakeholder management** by defining strategies to successfully engage stakeholders based on their influence, interest, and support
- **Manage stakeholder engagement** by working with stakeholders through the project lifecycle to ensure they are engaged in the project, as necessary, and their needs and expectations are met
- **Control stakeholder engagement** by monitoring and adjusting the stakeholder management plan, as appropriate

Knowledge Areas	Project Management Process Groups				
	Initiating Process Group	Planning Process Group	Executing Process Group	Monitoring and Controlling Process Group	Closing Process Group
Project Stakeholder Management	Identify Stakeholders	Plan Stakeholder Management	Manage Stakeholder Engagement	Control Stakeholder Engagement	

A stakeholder analysis may be used as an input to a lessons-learned plan or to the risk management plan. While your stakeholder management plan template may vary slightly, it will likely contain many of the components found in the following example. This image depicts a basic stakeholder management plan template, along with its elements.

Section 4: Project Management

Stakeholder Management Plan									
Project Name:					Project Manager:			Date:	
Who		What			How	Who	When	Other
Stakeholder	Stakeholder's Role	Influence High/Low	Interest High/Low	Support Neutral Against	Monitor Inform Satisfy Manage	Strategy	Strategy Owner	Strategy Date	Comments

Regardless of your stakeholder management template, format, and layout, it is essential – for larger and more complex projects – to include such a plan in the project toolbox and to review it during project review meetings.

Wishing you much success in your pursuit of stakeholder understanding and management, thereby generating greater value in your organization!

Work Breakdown Structure (WBS)

A work breakdown structure (WBS) is created early in the project planning process, after the project requirements have been completed. It is a detailed plan that breaks down the project into smaller components of product, information, or services, accounting for every activity essential for planning and executing the project.

A work breakdown structure is critical and necessary to the project lifecycle to:

- Identify and mitigate risks
- Define and manage controls
- Establish costs and track budgets
- Conduct planning and develop schedules
- Manage performance and track schedules
- Assign ownership and responsibilities to the project elements

Section 4: Project Management

Benefits of a work breakdown structure include:

- Save cost and time by defining and organizing project work
- Provide a consistent approach for efficiently planning and effectively executing a project
- Provide a visualization of the project scope and key deliverables in manageable activities
- Provide input to determine costs, budgets, resources, schedules, and responsibilities
- Provide input for identifying and managing potential risks and creating controls
- Provide a collaborative team environment

A work breakdown structure is constructed prior to conducting project work, and each level of the work breakdown structure (WBS) provides additional definition for the previous level. In a WBS, the project is the highest level; it is divided into tasks, sub-tasks, and work packages.

Key considerations when constructing a work breakdown structure include:

- Each level of the WBS is identified as a deliverable or outcome, rather than the work or actions necessary
- The termination – or lowest level – of the WBS has no activity or series of activities requiring more than one project reporting period to deliver
- The WBS is not a substitute for the project schedule or project action plan
- The WBS is a project document (artifact) – and is part of the project toolbox – following the change control process, if changes are necessary

Work Breakdown Structure Process:

1. Assemble the project team and key stakeholders who have completed pre-work by reviewing available documents, such as the contract, statement of work (SOW), project charter, requirements document
2. Document the project title at the top of the work breakdown structure on the electronic template or using Post-it® notes on butcher

Section 4: Project Management

block paper
3. For Level 1 tasks, document 100 percent of the project deliverables, as defined in the pre-work documents
4. Decompose the Level 1 project deliverables into Level 2 subtasks, which can be completed and delivered by one or more team members, within a defined period appropriate for the size and complexity of the project
5. Further decompose the Level 2 subtasks into Level 3 work packages, which may be completed and delivered by a single resource within one project reporting period
6. Add the WBS to the project toolbox as input to additional project plans and schedules

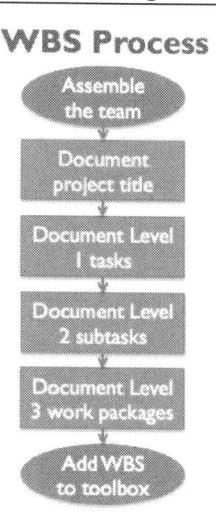

WBS Process

- Assemble the team
- Document project title
- Document Level 1 tasks
- Document Level 2 subtasks
- Document Level 3 work packages
- Add WBS to toolbox

Note: You may wish to reference PMBOK® 5th Edition for PMI® processes that make up the knowledge area for project scope management, specifically work breakdown structure (WBS). **Create WBS** by dividing project deliverables and work into tasks, sub-tasks, and work packages.

Knowledge Areas	Project Management Process Groups				
	Initiating Process Group	Planning Process Group	Executing Process Group	Monitoring and Controlling Process Group	Closing Process Group
Project Scope Management		Plan Scope Management Collect Requirements Define Scope Create WBS		Validate Scope Control Scope	

A work breakdown structure is used as an input to the resource plan, project schedule, action plan, and risk management plan. While your WBS template may vary slightly, it will likely contain many of the components found in the following example. This image depicts a basic work breakdown structure template in a tabular view, along with its elements. A work breakdown structure may also be defined in a tree view.

Section 4: Project Management

Work Breakdown Structure

Project Name:		
Project Manager:		Date:
Level 1	**Level 2**	**Level 3**
Task 1		
	Subtask 1.1	
		Work Package 1.1.1
		Work Package 1.1.2
		Work Package 1.1.3
	Subtask 1.2	
		Work Package 1.2.1
		Work Package 1.2.2
		Work Package 1.2.3
Task 2		
	Subtask 2.1	
		Work Package 2.1.1
		Work Package 2.1.2
		Work Package 2.1.3

Regardless of your work breakdown structure template, format, and layout, it is fundamental for larger and more complex projects to include a WBS in the project toolbox.

Wishing you much success in your pursuit of work breakdown, thereby generating greater value in your organization!

Resource Plan

A well-managed project resource plan – throughout the project lifecycle – is essential to the team's success in executing the project. Henry Ford is quoted as saying, "Coming together is a beginning. Keeping together is progress. Working together is success." The project resource plan is the beginning of forming your project team and leads to the success of your project.

Section 4: Project Management

A project resource plan may be used when:

- Resources are expected to be added and released during an active project lifecycle
- A project's size and complexity are such that a team of cross-functional resources is necessary
- A project enters the planning phase and ends when the project is closed, resources are released, and successes are celebrated

Benefits of a project resource plan include:

- Increase focus and attention on project team resources
- Provide an approach for efficiently and effectively forming the project team
- Provide a collaborative team environment
- Provide a consistent approach for managing project resource requirements

Project Resource Plan Process:

1. Determine project team roles and the resources required for the project, using project charter, requirements plan, and schedule; this is an iterative process conducted in the project planning phase, with some revisions in the execution, monitor, and control phases

   Resource Plan Process

   Determine resources required → Acquire resources
   ↓ ↓
   Determine start and end dates → Assign status
   ↓ ↓
   Determine total hours → Develop and manage

   a. Inputs to a resource plan may include the project charter, requirements document, work breakdown structure, project schedule, and action plan
2. Determine start and end dates for each project team member role and resource
3. Determine total hours required for each project team member role and resource
4. Work with resource managers to acquire necessary resources for the project
5. Assign status to each project team resource – Active, Not Needed, Not Started, Released, or Replaced
6. Develop and manage the project team

Section 4: Project Management

Note: You may wish to reference PMBOK® 5th Edition for PMI® processes that make up the knowledge area for project human resource management:

- **Plan human resource management** by recognizing and detailing project roles, responsibilities, required skills, reporting relationships, and creating a staffing management plan
- **Acquire project team** by working with sponsors and stakeholders to obtain human resources necessary to execute project activities
- **Develop project team** by improving team member skills and collaborations to enrich project performance
- **Manage project team** by tracking performance, providing feedback, and resolving issues to optimize project results

Knowledge Areas	Project Management Process Groups					
	Initiating Process Group	Planning Process Group	Executing Process Group	Monitoring and Controlling Process Group	Closing Process Group
Project Human Resource Management		Plan Human Resource Management	Acquire Project Team Develop Project Team Manage Project Team		

A resource plan may be used as an input to the communication plan, risk management plan, and lessons learned plan. While your project resource plan template may vary slightly, it will likely contain many of the components found in the following example. This image depicts a basic project resource plan template, along with its elements.

VALUE GENERATION PARTNERS	Project Resource Plan							
Project Name:			Project Manager:				Date:	
Who		What			When			Other
Name	Role	Department		Start Date	End Date	Total Hours	Status	Comments

Section 4: Project Management

Regardless of your project resource plan template, format, and layout, it is fundamental for larger and more complex projects to include such a plan in the project toolbox.

Wishing you much success in your pursuit of effectively resourcing your projects, thereby generating greater value in your organization!

Contact List

Have you ever been on a project and it seemed you were constantly looking for team member or stakeholder contact information? A contact list is a simple artifact that may be prepared early in the project and included in the project toolbox, eliminating frustration and waste caused by repeatedly seeking out this information. While a contact list is helpful for the effective and efficient execution of a project, it is very useful for other endeavors in business and may be considered for any undertaking.

A contact list can be helpful when:

- Project stakeholders and team members span many regions and time zones
- Project team and stakeholders are not co-located
- Project team's network is large and complex
- Project impacts safety, quality, or customer service
- Project requires significant communication and interaction between the team and stakeholders

Benefits of a contact list include:

- Provide a document that efficiently and effectively details names, email addresses, phone numbers of persons important to the project
- Save cost and time with quick access to contact information

While your contact list template may vary slightly, it will likely contain many of the components found in the following example. This image depicts a basic contact list template, along with its elements.

Section 4: Project Management

Project Name:						Project Manager:			
Last Name	First Name	Title	Role	Company	Location	Office Phone	Cell Phone	Email	Time Zone

Regardless of your contact list template, format, and layout, it is a great tool to include in the project toolbox to ensure efficient access to project-related contacts.

Wishing you much success in contact management, thereby generating greater value in your organization!

Schedule and Gantt Chart

A foundational and critical tool for managing the project lifecycle is a detailed project schedule. A well-developed and -executed project schedule – through all phases of the project lifecycle – is essential to every project's success. Any size and complexity of project will benefit from a project schedule. It is used when a project requires a few to any number of activities to complete deliverables.

Benefits of a project schedule include:

- Increase focus and attention on project deliverables and milestones
- Provide an approach for efficiently and effectively managing project activities
- Save cost and time by identifying, prioritizing, and managing project activities
- Provide a consistent approach for analyzing, prioritizing, communicating, and managing project activities
- Provide a collaborative team environment

Section 4: Project Management

Project schedule includes:

- Milestones and activities
- Dependencies
- Duration of each activity (in days)
- Resources assigned to each activity
- Percentage complete for each activity (in increments of 0%, 10%, 20%, etc.)
- Status – On Schedule, Ahead of Schedule, Behind Schedule, Complete, or Not Started
- Start and finish dates for each activity
- Comments

Project Schedule Process:

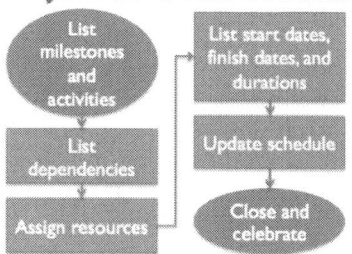

1. List project milestones and activities necessary to complete during the project lifecycle
   a. Inputs to the project schedule may include the project charter, requirements document, and work breakdown structure
2. List dependencies for each activity
   a. Finish to Start – predecessor must finish before successor can start; software must be deployed before it can be maintained
   b. Start to Start – predecessor must start before successor can start; software coding must start before testing can begin
   c. Finish to Finish – predecessor must finish before successor can finish; software design must finish before coding can finish
   d. Start to Finish – predecessor must start before successor can finish; software design must start before coding can finish
3. Assign a resource for each activity
4. Define start date, finish date, and duration for each activity
5. Update the project schedule when

Section 4: Project Management

     a. Percent complete changes for a given activity, such as 0%, 10%, 20%, ... 100%
     b. Status changes for a given activity, such as On Schedule, Ahead of Schedule, Behind Schedule, Complete, or Not Started
     c. New milestones or activities are identified
     d. Project scope or resources change
6. Close the project and celebrate project completion

Note: You may wish to reference PMBOK® 5th Edition for PMI® processes that make up the knowledge area for project time management:

- **Plan schedule management** by developing documentation for planning, defining, implementing, and controlling the project schedule
- **Define activities** by defining and documenting precise activities necessary to produce project deliverables
- **Sequence activities** by defining and documenting the relationships and order of project activities
- **Estimate activity resources** by determining team members, supplies, materials, and equipment necessary to execute project activities
- **Estimate activity durations** by determining time requirements needed to complete each activity based on estimated resources
- **Develop schedule** by evaluating activity sequences, resource requirements, durations, and schedule constraints to create the project schedule
- **Control schedule** by monitoring, updating, and managing the status of project activities and progress to achieve the project plan

Knowledge Areas	Project Management Process Groups					
	Initiating Process Group	Planning Process Group	Executing Process Group	Monitoring and Controlling Process Group	Closing Process Group
Project Time Management		Plan Schedule Management Define Activities Sequence Activities Estimate Activity Resources Estimate Activity Durations Develop Schedule		Control Schedule	

Section 4: Project Management

Most project schedules include a graphical depiction of the timeline in the form of a Gantt chart. Many of the project scheduling software packages generate a Gantt chart as a result of inputting the project schedule's start date, finish date, dependencies, and duration. However, if you wish to create a Gantt chart manually as part of a project schedule, you will typically use the symbols depicted in the following image.

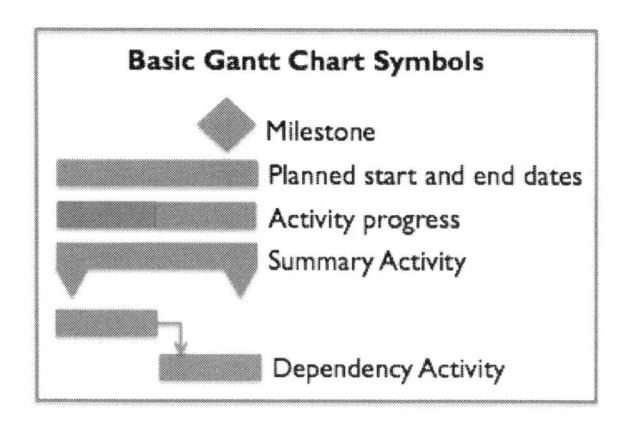

Basic Gantt Chart Symbols

- ◆ Milestone
- ▬ Planned start and end dates
- ▬ Activity progress
- ▽ Summary Activity
- ▬ Dependency Activity

A project schedule may be used as an input to the resource plan, communication plan, risk management plan, and lessons learned plan. While your project schedule template may vary slightly, it will likely contain many of the components found in the following example. This image depicts a project schedule template, along with its elements. While this image is created in a spreadsheet format, a project schedule may also be created using a project management software package.

Section 4: Project Management

Project Schedule

Name	Dependency	Days	Resource	Percent	Status	Start	Finish	Comments
Total Timeline		72		0.00%	On Schedule	4/14/15	6/25/15	
Initiate		10		0.00%	On Schedule	4/14/15	4/24/15	
Create Project Charter		6		0.00%	On Schedule	4/14/15	4/20/15	
Identify Stakeholders		4		0.00%	On Schedule	4/16/15	4/20/15	
Review Project Charter with Stakeholders		2		0.00%	On Schedule	4/20/15	4/22/15	
Project Charter Approved		2		0.00%	On Schedule	4/22/15	4/24/15	
Plan		22		0.00%	On Schedule	4/24/15	5/16/15	
Facilitate Project Kick-Off		2		0.00%	On Schedule	4/24/15	4/26/15	
Collect Requirements		5		0.00%	On Schedule	4/26/15	5/1/15	
Define Project Scope		2		0.00%	On Schedule	5/1/15	5/3/15	
Create Work Breakdown Structure		3		0.00%	On Schedule	5/3/15	5/6/15	
Create Project Schedule		3		0.00%	On Schedule	5/6/15	5/9/15	
Create Resource Plan		2		0.00%	On Schedule	5/9/15	5/11/15	
Create Project Financial Report		4		0.00%	On Schedule	5/9/15	5/13/15	
Create Communication Plan		4		0.00%	On Schedule	5/9/15	5/13/15	
Create Stakeholder Management Plan		3		0.00%	On Schedule	5/9/15	5/12/15	
Create Risk Management Plan		4		0.00%	On Schedule	5/9/15	5/13/15	
Create Change Management Plan		3		0.00%	On Schedule	5/9/15	5/12/15	
Begin Project Status Reporting								
Conduct Lessons Learned		3		0.00%	On Schedule	5/13/15	5/16/15	
Execute		33		0.00%	On Schedule	5/9/15	6/11/15	
Form and Develop Project Team		5		0.00%	On Schedule	5/9/15	5/14/15	
Execute and Manage Project Work and Team (List steps in this phase)		25		0.00%	On Schedule	5/14/15	6/8/15	
- Execution Steps for Project Deliverables, Quality, Communications								
Conduct Lessons Learned		3		0.00%	On Schedule	6/8/15	6/11/15	
Monitor and Control		51		0.00%	On Schedule	4/24/15	6/14/15	
Conduct Monitor and Controls (List steps in this phase)		48		0.00%	On Schedule	4/24/15	6/11/15	
- Change Control, Scope, Costs, Quality, Communications, Risks, Stakeholders								
Conduct Lessons Learned		3		0.00%	On Schedule	6/11/15	6/14/15	
Close		11		0.00%	On Schedule	6/14/15	6/25/15	
Close Project Financials		5		0.00%	On Schedule	6/14/15	6/19/15	
Conduct Lessons Learned		3		0.00%	On Schedule	6/19/15	6/22/15	
Project Close and Sign-off		3		0.00%	On Schedule	6/22/15	6/25/15	
Release Resources		0		0.00%	On Schedule	6/25/15	6/25/15	
Celebration		0		0.00%	On Schedule	6/25/15	6/25/15	

Regardless of your project schedule template, format, and layout, it is fundamental for larger and more complex projects to include such a schedule in the project toolbox and to review it during project review meetings.

Wishing you much success in your pursuit of managing the project schedule, thereby generating greater value in your organization!

Communication Plan

A critical artifact to include in the project toolbox and during the lifecycle of the project is a communication plan. A well-executed communication plan – through all phases of the project lifecycle – is essential to the success of the project. While a communication plan is critical to the success of project execution, it is equally important for all endeavors in business and should be considered for any under- taking. A communication plan may be used by department managers

Section 4: Project Management

to effectively lead, by executives to deploy strategies, and for execution of any type of change initiative.

Anthony Robbins is credited with the quote, "Skill in the art of communication is crucial to a leader's success; one can accomplish nothing unless one can communicate effectively." And George Bernard Shaw was quoted as saying, "The single biggest problem in communication is the illusion that it has taken place." Both quotes signify the importance of a well-developed and well-executed communication plan, regardless of its intended use.

Benefits of a project communication plan include:

- Facilitates securing support for your project
- Socialization and clarification of the project charter
- Clarification of roles and responsibilities
- Status and health (scope, schedule, and budget) of the project
- Updates on project issues, risks, and changes
- Updates on project activities, implementation plans, and training plans

Communication Plan development and maintenance process:

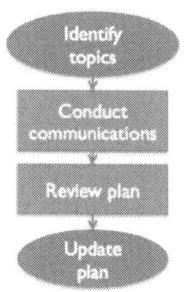

1. Project manager, with input from sponsor and team, makes communication topic entries on the communication plan template
    a. Inputs to the communication plan topics and entries may include project charter, project schedule, stakeholder management plan, resource plan, quality management plan, risk management plan, issue management plan, change control plan, training plan, and project close
2. Communication topic owners conduct communications, as described on the communication plan
3. Project manager reviews the communication plan with team during project review meetings
4. New communication topic entries or adjustments are entered in the plan and reviewed during project review meetings

Communication Plan Process

- Identify topics
- Conduct communications
- Review plan
- Update plan

Section 4: Project Management

Note: You may wish to reference PMBOK® 5th Edition for PMI® processes that make up the knowledge area for project communication management:

- **Plan communication management** by developing a communication plan based on stakeholder input and needs
- **Manage communications** by creating, distributing, collecting, and storing project communications
- **Control communications** by ensuring stakeholders' communications needs are met through the project lifecycle

Knowledge Areas	Project Management Process Groups				
	Initiating Process Group	Planning Process Group	Executing Process Group	Monitoring and Controlling Process Group	Closing Process Group
Project Communication Management		Plan Communication Management	Manage Communications	Control Communications	

Communication plan templates may vary based on your organization and needs; however, most will contain components found in the following example. This image depicts a basic communication plan template, along with its elements.

Communication Plan

Project Name:					Project Manager:		
Who		What	When		Why	Where/How	Other
Owner	Audience	Topic	Timing		Intent	Delivery Channel	Comments

Regardless of your communication plan template, format, and layout, it is essential to include such a plan in the project toolbox and to review it during project review meetings.

Wishing you much success in your pursuit of planning effective communications, thereby generating greater value in your organization!

Section 4: Project Management

Informative Communication

Rather far, relatively short, very small, extremely heavy, fairly new, too many, very long, pretty old, oversized, a lot, completely under-sized, too few, quite large, very late. In everyday conversation, these words are perfectly fine, yet in defining strategies or projects for Operational Excellence, these words are not truly informative.

So, why do I suggest these words are not informative, when they're used all the time? Have you ever attended a project report-out meeting that went something like this? "The process takes way too long, so we are going to shorten it a lot." You would most certainly say that was not informative. Obviously I'm kidding; no experienced project manager would use these words to describe a process or a project, however it is important to instill a culture of clear communication and informative reporting.

Let's explore an example of using non-informational words in everyday life:

- There are a lot of people ahead of us in line at the movie ticket counter.

What is meant by "a lot" of people? Is it five, 10, or more? A lot can mean different things to different people, or even different things to the same person based on varying circumstances. If I arrive at the ticket counter just as the movie is about to begin, then a lot of people might very well be five; yet if I arrive at the ticket counter 15 minutes before the movie is about to start, a lot may be a dozen. A lot to you might be 15; for me, under the same circumstances, a lot might be six.

Let's explore some other examples:

- I can't make it to the store and back home in time for the movie, because it's extremely far.
    - How far is the store from the house – two miles, 10 miles, more than 25 miles?
- My car is considered a classic because it's very old.
    - How old is the car – five years, 15 years, 50 years?
- I can't lift these boxes, because they're awfully heavy.

Section 4: Project Management

- - How heavy are the boxes – five pounds, 50 pounds, more than 100 pounds?
- Please don't leave without me; I'll be there <u>soon</u>.
  - How soon will you be – an hour, 30 minutes, 15 minutes or less?

What if the sentences were written like this?

- I can't make it to the store and back home in time for the movie, because it's <u>10 miles one way</u>.
- My car is considered a classic, because it's <u>35 years old</u>.
- I can't lift these boxes, because they're <u>more than 100 pounds each</u>.
- Please don't leave without me; I'll be there in <u>20 minutes</u>.

Do the rewritten sentences provide more factual and useful information? Great! So let's get back to Operational Excellence and informative reporting. When defining strategies, writing a project charter, writing a project summary, or reporting out the status of an improvement initiative, take the time to be informative and factual with your words. You will generate a greater understanding of and stronger support for your efforts.

Wishing you much success in clearly and factually – informatively – communicating, thereby generating greater value in your organization!

Concise Communications

In the interest of this chapter's topic, I'll keep it concise – meaning it will be brief, yet comprehensive. Concise reporting, presentations, and writing are as important in transformation and operational excellence, as in any other field of practice. Concise communication carries forward in the documentation of a project description or goal, a project report, and a project presentation for a group of stakeholders.

I imagine you can remember a presentation you attended or a report you received that went on, and on, and on, and on? These types of run-on communications tend to leave us more confused than informed. It is possible to be brief and to convey important information, as seen in the important works of the Pythagorean Theorem, referenced in 24 words, and Archimedes' Principle, referenced in 67 words. Even Chinese proverbs are famous for being short, and chock-full of wisdom.

As you coach and mentor your project managers in continuous improvement methodologies, you may also include discussion and training around concise reporting. Train them to determine the objective of the communication, to know their audience, and to plan accordingly. Project managers should understand that the first few minutes or words of a communication are critical; they need to convey the important message and hook the audience. Project managers should spend time reviewing, practicing, and refining their reports and presentations to find the perfect balance between detail and brevity, thereby meeting the intent of concise reporting.

Wishing you much success in your pursuit of communication with clarity and brevity, and being concise, thereby generating greater value in your organization!

Quality Management Plan

The project quality management plan, a necessary artifact to include in the project toolbox, is critical to the success of the project lifecycle and its deliverables. William A. Foster – physicist, businessman, and politician – is attributed with the quote, "Quality is never an accident; it is always the result of high intention, sincere effort, intelligent direction, and skillful execution; it represents the wise choice of many alternatives."

Likely any project being chartered and initiated will necessitate a project quality management plan. However, if the project meets any of the following criteria, you must create one:

Section 4: Project Management

- Project results in a new process, product, or service
- Project impacts safety, quality, or customer service
- Project is managed for scope, schedule, and budget
- Project has defined deliverables and metrics for success criteria

Benefits of a project quality management plan include:

- Increase focus and attention on project quality
- Provide an improved starting point for future projects
- Provide an approach to ensure project requirements are met
- Save cost and time by identifying and controlling project quality
- Provide a consistent approach for identifying and controlling project quality

Project Quality Management Plan Process:

1. Identify quality management needs
    a. Inputs to project quality management plan may include project charter, work breakdown structure, project schedule, stakeholder management plan, resource plan, procurement management plan, risk management plan, issue management plan, change control plan
2. Document each quality characteristic and reason
3. Assign quality type – Customer, Deliverable, Process, Product, Project, Regulatory, Service
4. Document timing, method, and quality owner
5. Review during project review meetings and assign each quality characteristic a status – Cancelled, Closed, In-Process, Not Started, Open
6. Close the quality management plan, when complete

Note: You may wish to reference PMBOK® 5th Edition for PMI® processes that make up the knowledge area of project quality management:

Section 4: Project Management

- **Plan quality management** by identifying quality requirements and compliance reporting for the project and its deliverables
- **Perform quality assurance** by monitoring quality results and ensuring quality requirements are being followed and met
- **Control quality** by monitoring, recording, reporting, and taking action on the results of project quality activities

Knowledge Areas	Project Management Process Groups				
	Initiating Process Group	Planning Process Group	Executing Process Group	Monitoring and Controlling Process Group	Closing Process Group
Project Quality Management		Plan Quality Management	Perform Quality Assurance	Control Quality	

While your project quality management plan template may vary slightly, it will likely contain many of the components found in the following example. This image depicts a basic project quality management plan template, along with its elements.

Quality Management Plan						
Project Name:			Project Manager:		Date:	
What	Why	When	How	Who	What	Other
Characteristic	Type	Reason	Timing	Method	Owner	Status	Comments

Regardless of your project quality management plan template, format, and layout; it is useful to include such a plan in the project toolbox and to review it during project review meetings.

Wishing you much success in your pursuit of project quality management, thereby generating greater value in your organization!

Section 4: Project Management

Procurement Management Plan

A project procurement management plan may be a necessary artifact to include in the project toolbox, if procurement is required as part of the project lifecycle. Create a project procurement management plan when the project requires procurement – of consulting, hardware, labor, materials, maintenance, service, software, or tooling – to execute the project.

Benefits of a project procurement management plan include:

- Increase focus and attention on project procurement activities and status
- Save cost and time by managing project procurement activities and status
- Provide a consistent approach for efficiently and effectively managing project procurement

Project Procurement Management Plan Process:

1. Identify procurement needs
    a. Inputs to project procurement management plan may include project charter, work breakdown structure, project schedule, stakeholder management plan, resource plan, quality management plan, risk management plan, issue management plan, change control plan, training plan
2. Document each procurement description and reason
3. Assign procurement type – Consulting, Contractor, Hardware, Labor, Materials, Maintenance, Service, Software, Tooling
4. Document procurement owner and timing of the need
5. Review during project review meetings and assign procurement status – Cancelled, Closed, In-Process, Not Started, Open
6. Close procurement management plan when complete

Section 4: Project Management

Note: You may wish to reference PMBOK® 5th Edition for PMI® processes that make up the knowledge area of project procurement management:

- **Plan procurement management** by defining the project procurement conclusions, specifying the approach, and identifying potential suppliers
- **Conduct procurement** by obtaining quotes, selecting suppliers, and granting contracts
- **Control procurement** by measuring and managing performance to purchasing and contract requirements
- **Close procurement** by completing purchasing contract requirements

Knowledge Areas	Project Management Process Groups					
	Initiating Process Group	Planning Process Group	Executing Process Group	Monitoring and Controlling Process Group	Closing Process Group
Project Procurement Management		Plan Procurement Management	Conduct Procurement	Control Procurement	Close Procurement

While your project procurement management plan template may vary slightly, it will likely contain many of the components found in the following example. This image depicts a basic project procurement management plan template, along with its elements.

VALUE GENERATION PARTNERS — Procurement Management Plan

Project Name:					
Project Manager:				Date:	
What	Why	When	Who	What	Other
Description	Type	Reason	Timing	Owner	Status	Comments

Regardless of your project procurement management plan template, format, and layout; it is useful to include such a plan in the project

107

Section 4: Project Management

toolbox any time procurements are required during the project lifecycle and to review it during project review meetings.

Wishing you much success in your pursuit of project procurement management, thereby generating greater value in your organization!

Risk Management Plan

Every project contains some level and amount of risk. To manage and mitigate project risks, include the risk management plan as a key artifact in the project toolbox, especially when managing complex projects. Theodore Roosevelt said, "Risk is like fire: If controlled it will help you; if uncontrolled it will rise up and destroy you." A well-executed risk management plan – through all phases of the project lifecycle – is essential to the success of the project. While a risk management plan is critical to the success of project execution, it is very useful for other endeavors in business and may be considered for any undertaking.

Unlike issues, risks are not yet directly impacting the project and may be mitigated and prevented from turning into an issue. Should a risk turn into an issue, it will be more time consuming and costly to recover from than the original risk, had it been mitigated.

A risk management plan may be used when the project:

- Results in a new process, product, or service
- Impacts safety, quality, or customer service
- Is large, complex, and costly

Benefits of a risk management plan include:

- Increase focus and attention on risks
- Proactive approach for preventing risks from becoming issues
- Provide a consistent approach for analyzing, prioritizing, communicating, and managing risks
- Provide an approach to efficiently and effectively mitigate risks
- Save cost and time by identifying, prioritizing, and managing risks

Section 4: Project Management

The risk management process defined below is an ideal approach for managing and mitigating risks.

Risk Management Plan Process:

1. A risk is identified during the project lifecycle
   a. Inputs to the risk management plan may include project charter, project schedule, stakeholder management plan, resource plan, quality management plan, issue management plan, change control plan, communication plan, and training plan
2. Risk is logged on the risk management plan template
3. Project team assesses and prioritizes the risk based on probability and impact to project health, scope, schedule, and budget
4. Project team determines response type (accept, avoid, reduce, or transfer) and response plan to mitigate the risk
5. Project team monitors and controls the risk via the response plan
6. Process is repeated when additional risks are identified

Risk Management Process
- Risks identified
- Logged and assessed
- Prioritized and response type
- Monitor and control
- Status (Open/Mitigated)
- Close risk plan

Note: You may wish to reference PMBOK® 5th Edition for PMI® processes that make up the knowledge area for project risk management:

- **Plan risk management** by defining how the project team will conduct risk management
- **Identify risks** by defining and documenting risks that may affect the project
- **Perform qualitative risk analysis** by prioritizing risks for further analysis and action based on probability and impact
- **Perform quantitative risk analysis** by analyzing and ranking risks for effect on project objectives
- **Plan risk response** by developing actions to mitigate the dangers to the project objectives
- **Control risks** by implementing the risk response plan, tracking risk status, and identifying and managing new risks

Section 4: Project Management

Knowledge Areas	Project Management Process Groups				
	Initiating Process Group	Planning Process Group	Executing Process Group	Monitoring and Controlling Process Group	Closing Process Group
Project Risk Management		Plan Risk Management Identify Risks Perform Qualitative Risk Analysis Perform Quantitative Risk Analysis Plan Risk Response		Control Risks	

A risk management plan may be used as input to a lessons learned plan. While your risk management plan template may vary slightly, it will likely contain many of the components found in the following example. This image depicts a basic risk management plan template, along with its elements.

Regardless of your risk management plan template, format, and layout, it is important for larger and more complex projects to include such a plan in the project toolbox and to review it during project review meetings.

Wishing you much success in your pursuit of risk management and mitigation, thereby generating greater value in your organization!

Section 4: Project Management

Issue Management Plan

Issues are likely to come up during the lifecycle of a project, and an issue management plan is a necessary artifact to include in the project toolbox. These plans are effective for handling complex projects – specifically to manage and recover from issues. Author Susan Del Gatto said, "If you choose to not deal with an issue, then you give up your right of control over the issue and it will select the path of least resistance." A well-executed issue management plan – through all phases of the project lifecycle – is essential to the success of the project. While an issue management plan is critical to the success of project execution, it is very useful for other endeavors in business and may be considered for any undertaking.

Issues are typically unexpected, and many times must be dealt with quickly, to ensure the health of the project – for scope, schedule, and budget. Unlike risks, issues exist and must be managed; however, a solid risk management plan may help prevent some risks from becoming issues.

An issue management plan should be used when issues present themselves during the project lifecycle.

Benefits of an issue management plan include:

- Increase focus and attention on issues
- Provide a consistent approach for analyzing, prioritizing, communicating, and managing issues
- Provide an approach for efficiently and effectively resolving issues
- Provide a collaborative and team environment
- Save cost and time by identifying, prioritizing, and managing issues

The issue management process defined below is an ideal approach for managing issues.

Issue Management Plan Process:

1. An issue is identified during the project lifecycle

Section 4: Project Management

2. The issue is logged and prioritized on the issue management plan template
3. The project team analyzes the issue for source and cause, along with impact to the project health, for scope, schedule, and budget
4. The project team develops a recovery plan for the issue
5. The project team monitors and reviews the issue to ensure that the recovery plan has been successful
6. The process is repeated when any additional issues are identified

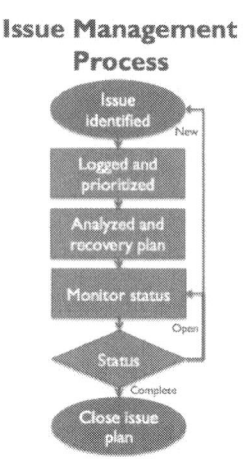

Issue Management Process

- Issue identified (New)
- Logged and prioritized
- Analyzed and recovery plan
- Monitor status (Open)
- Status (Complete)
- Close issue plan

An issue management plan may be used as an input to a lessons learned plan or to the risk management plan. While your issue management plan template may vary slightly, it will likely contain many of the components found in the following example. This image depicts a basic issue management plan template, along with its elements.

VALUE GENERATIONPARTNERS — Issue Management Plan

Project Name:
Project Manager:

#	When	What			Who	How	When		Other
	Date Raised	Issue Description	Priority	Impact	Issue Owner	Recovery Plan	Due Date	Issue Status	Comments
1									
2									
3									
4									
5									
6									
7									

Regardless of your issue management plan template, format, and layout, it is fundamental for larger and more complex projects to include such a plan in the project toolbox and to review it during project review meetings.

Wishing you much success in your pursuit of issue management and resolution, thereby generating greater value in your organization!

Section 4: Project Management

Change Control Plan

A change control plan is a key artifact to include in the project toolbox and during the lifecycle of complex projects to manage and document project change requests. A well-managed change control plan – through all phases of the project lifecycle – is essential to the success of the project. While change control is critical to the success of project execution, it is very useful for other endeavors in business and should be considered for any undertaking susceptible to change.

Charles Darwin has been attributed to several variations of this quote: "It is not the strongest nor the most intelligent who will survive, but those who can best manage change." In today's fast-paced environment, change is inevitable, and in order to align with customer and business needs, it is likely that a project will encounter change requests at some point in the project lifecycle.

A change control plan shall be used when changes are requested by any of the project's stakeholders; changes are normal occurrences – and may happen more than once – in the project lifecycle.

Benefits of a change control plan include:

- Provide a consistent approach for analyzing, prioritizing, communicating, and managing changes
- Provide an approach for efficiently and effectively adapting to change
- Proactive approach to preparing for change
- Save cost and time by identifying, prioritizing, and managing changes
- Provide a collaborative team environment

To ensure each change request is defined, evaluated, accepted or rejected, and executed properly, a change control process is essential. The change control process will ensure that resources are utilized efficiently and customers, processes, and services are not disrupted unnecessarily.

Section 4: Project Management

Change Control Plan Process:

1. Project manager receives a change request
2. Project manager clarifies and documents the change request on the change control plan template
3. Project manager and team analyze change request and determine impact to project scope, schedule, or budget
4. Project manager, team, and sponsor accept or reject – disposition – the change request; this step may be performed by a change control board
5. Project manager notifies the change requestor of disposition – acceptance or rejection
6. Project manager documents the change request disposition on the change control plan template
7. Project manager and team re-baseline the project based on the change request impact
8. Project manager and team manage the project based on the new baseline, incorporating the change

Change Control Process

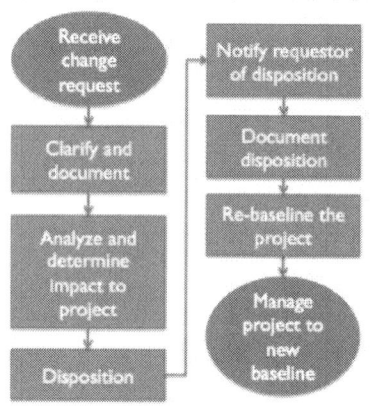

Receive change request → Notify requestor of disposition → Document disposition → Re-baseline the project → Manage project to new baseline

Clarify and document → Analyze and determine impact to project → Disposition

Note: You may wish to reference PMBOK® 5th Edition for PMI® processes making up the knowledge area for project integration management, specifically perform integrated change control. **Perform integrated change control** by reviewing project change requests and adjusting project schedules, plans, and deliverables based on disposition and impact.

Knowledge Areas	Project Management Process Groups					
	Initiating Process Group	Planning Process Group	Executing Process Group	Monitoring and Controlling Process Group	Closing Process Group
Project Integration Management	Develop Project Charter	Develop Project Management Plan	Direct and Manage Project Work	Monitor and Control Project Work; Perform Integrated Change Control	Close Project or Phase

Section 4: Project Management

A change control plan may be used as an input to a lessons learned plan or to the risk management plan. While your change control plan template may vary slightly, it will likely contain many of the components found in the following example. This image depicts a basic change control plan template, along with its elements.

	Who	What	When	Who	What		When	Other
#	Requested By	Change Requested	Request Date	Reviewed By	Priority	Impact	Status	Decision Date	Comments
1									
2									
3									
4									
5									
6									
7									

Project Name: Project Manager:

(Change Control Plan)

Regardless of your change control plan template, format, and layout, it is vital for larger and more complex projects to include such a plan in the project toolbox and to review it during project review meetings.

Wishing you much success in your pursuit of change control management, thereby generating greater value in your organization!

Lessons-Learned Plan

A lessons-learned plan, a necessary artifact to include in the project toolbox, is typically captured and acted upon during all phases of the project lifecycle. Lessons are later transferred to a lessons-learned repository for access and use on other projects. "It's fine to celebrate success, but it is more important to heed the lessons of failure," said Bill Gates. A well-executed lessons-learned plan – through all phases of the project lifecycle – is essential to the success of the project. While a lessons-learned plan is critical to the success of project execution, it is very useful for other endeavors in business, and may be considered for many undertakings.

The following are some typical lessons-learned questions:

1. What went well?
2. What could have gone better?

Section 4: Project Management

3. What obstacles were encountered?
4. What processes need improved?
5. What risks were not managed and mitigated?
6. What was the project goal/objective and what was accomplished?
7. What other suggestions should be included in the lessons-learned plan?

Conduct a lessons-learned plan when:

- Project results in a new process, product, or service
- Project spans many groups, functions, or departments
- Project phases are complex or lengthy
- The project impacts safety, quality, or customer service

Benefits of a lessons-learned plan include:

- Promote continuous improvement
- Provide an improved starting point for future projects
- Provide a consistent approach for identifying, prioritizing, and acting upon lessons learned
- Enhance a collaborative team environment
- Save cost and time by identifying, prioritizing, and acting upon lessons learned

The lessons-learned plan process, defined below, is an ideal approach for documenting lessons learned and realizing future benefits, as a result of conducting this exercise.

Lessons-Learned Plan Process:

1. Notify and prepare the project team members for the lessons-learned session
2. Facilitate lessons-learned brainstorming sessions throughout the lifecycle of the project
    a. Inputs to a lessons-learned plan may include project charter, project schedule, stakeholder management plan, communication plan, resource plan, quality management plan, risk man-

Lessons-Learned Process

Assemble the team → Determine action plan
Conduct session → Take action and follow-up
Log, categorize, and prioritize lessons learned → Add to repository

Section 4: Project Management

agement plan, issue management plan, change control plan, training plan, and project close
3. Project team logs, categorizes, and prioritizes lessons learned on the lessons-learned plan template
4. Project team determines an action plan (who, what, and when) for each lesson learned
5. Project team reviews all of the lessons learned to ensure the action plan has been successfully executed
6. Closed and completed lessons-learned actions are added to the intellectual-asset repository

While your lessons-learned plan template may vary slightly, it will likely contain many of the components found in the following example. This image depicts a basic lessons-learned plan template, along with its elements.

VALUE GENERATION PARTNERS		Lessons-Learned Plan						
Project Name:						Project Manager:		
When	What			Who	How	When	What	Other
Date	Lesson Description	Category	Priority	Owner	Lesson Action	Date	Status	Comments

Regardless of your lessons-learned plan template, format, and layout; it is useful to include such a plan in the project toolbox and to review it during project review meetings.

Wishing you much success in your pursuit of continuous improvement through identifying, documenting, and following up on lessons learned, thereby generating greater value in your organization!

Checklist

A project checklist is another useful artifact to include in the project toolbox. It is effective for handling complex projects – specifically to manage the ownership of the many templates, logs, and plans necessary to complete the project lifecycle. Atul Gawande, author of The

Section 4: Project Management

Checklist Manifesto: How to Get Things Right, is quoted as saying, "Good checklists, on the other hand, are precise. They are efficient, to the point, and easy to use even in the most difficult situations. Good checklists are, above all, practical." While a project checklist leads to the success of project governance and execution, checklists may be applied in other endeavors in business and may be considered for any undertaking.

A project checklist may be helpful when:

- Project requires many templates, logs, and plans to be created throughout the project lifecycle
- Ownership of templates, logs, and plans is spread among various project team members
- The organizational system requires management and retention of project artifacts as intellectual assets

Benefits of a project checklist include:

- Provide ownership and timing of the creation of templates, logs, and plans
- Increase focus and attention on templates, logs, plans, and project governance
- Save cost and time by efficiently and effectively managing templates, logs, and plans
- Enhance a collaborative team environment

Project Checklist Process:

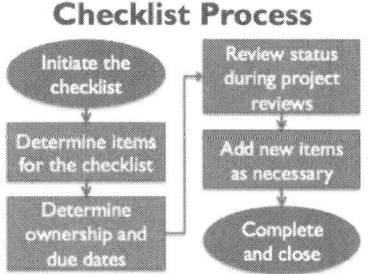

1. Initiate the project checklist in the early planning phase of project
2. Secure input from the project team and sponsor to determine which templates, logs, and plans are necessary to add to the project checklist
3. Work with project team to determine ownership and due dates for items identified on the project checklist
4. Review the checklist during project review meetings to determine

Checklist Process

- Initiate the checklist
- Determine items for the checklist
- Determine ownership and due dates
- Review status during project reviews
- Add new items as necessary
- Complete and close

Section 4: Project Management

status of checklist items
5. Add new items to the checklist, as necessary, throughout the project lifecycle
6. Complete the checklist as part of the project-close process

While your project checklist template may vary slightly, it will likely contain many of the components found in the following example. This image depicts a basic project checklist template, along with its elements.

VALUE GENERATION PARTNERS — Project Checklist

Project Name:							
Project Manager:				Date:			
What		When	Who	What		When	Other
Item or Template	Required	Date	Owner	Status		Date	Comments
Charter	Yes						
Requirements Document	Yes						
Financial Document	Yes						
Contact List	Yes						
Stakeholder Analysis	Yes						
Communication Plan	Yes						
Staffing Plan	Yes						
Work Breakdown Structure	Yes						
Schedule	Yes						
Action Plan	Yes						
Risk Management Plan	Yes						
Issue Management Plan	Yes						
Change Control Plan	Yes						
Lessons Learned Log	Yes						
SIPOC	Yes						
Process Map	No						
RACI	Yes						
Cause and Effect Diagram/Matrix	No						
Data Collection Plan	No						
Pugh Matrix	No						
Solution Selection Matrix	Yes						
Force Field Analysis	No						
Impact/Effort Matrix	No						
FMEA	No						
Training Plan	Yes						
Control Plan	Yes						
Status Report	Yes						
Close and Sign-off Document	Yes						
Celebration	Yes						

Regardless of your project checklist template, format, and layout, it is fundamental for larger and more complex projects to include such a checklist in the project toolbox and to review it during project review meetings.

Wishing you much success in your checklist management, thereby generating greater value in your organization!

Section 4: Project Management

Close-out and Sign-off

An exciting and rewarding time in the project lifecycle is the close. It's when you validate that the *t*'s have been crossed, the *i*'s have been dotted, and you celebrate the team's success. Team members are released and you move on to the next great project. Yet, before doing that ... celebrate!

A project-close process should be conducted at the completion of all chartered projects. It typically consists of completing the following steps:

1. Validate that products, processes, or services meet project scope, goals, and deliverables
2. Validate that processes, procedures, records, and training are updated and delivered
3. Confirm that products, processes, or services are delivered to the customer or sponsor
4. Secure acceptance of the products, processes, or services from the customer and/or sponsor
5. Ensure project team evaluations are complete and resources are released
6. Conduct final project review, document lessons learned and add to the intellectual-asset repository
7. Archive project documents and artifacts
8. Deliver final project report
9. Conduct a project team celebration

All of the project-close items in the list above are important and necessary, yet project team recognition and celebration are critical to the success of future projects and to enhance organizational culture. Recognition and celebration should provide positive reinforcement, in a setting instrumental to personal reward, and conducted or attended by leadership and senior management.

Benefits of project close:

- Provide a collaborative, motivational team environment
- Provide a smooth transition of ownership of deliverables
- Provide a consistent approach for efficiently and effectively closing projects

Section 4: Project Management

- Provide a basis for future projects to reference
- Result in a customer-centric approach and environment

The process defined below is an ideal approach for project close.

Project-Close Process:

1. Complete all activities on the project schedule and action plan
2. Complete all items on the project checklist
3. Complete the project-close and sign-off template
4. Conduct a project-close meeting with the appropriate stakeholders and sponsor
5. Secure project approval and sign-off
6. Recognize and celebrate the project team's success

Project-Close Process

Complete schedule and plan → Conduct project close meeting

Complete project close checklist → Secure approval and sign-off

Complete project close template → Recognize and celebrate

Note: You may wish to reference PMBOK® 5th Edition for PMI® processes that make up the knowledge area for project integration management, specifically close project or phase. **Close project or phase** by finalizing all activities and project work across all process groups necessary to formally complete the project or phase.

Knowledge Areas	Project Management Process Groups				
	Initiating Process Group	Planning Process Group	Executing Process Group	Monitoring and Controlling Process Group	Closing Process Group
Project Integration Management	Develop Project Charter	Develop Project Management Plan	Direct and Manage Project Work	Monitor and Control Project Work, Perform Integrated Change Control	Close Project or Phase

While your project-close and sign-off template may vary slightly, it will likely contain many of the components found in the following example. This image depicts a basic project-close and sign-off template, along with its elements.

121

Section 4: Project Management

Project Close and Sign-off

Project Name:	Close Date:	Project Number:
Project Sponsor:	Project Manager:	

- [ ] Final solution delivered and accepted
- [ ] Project team evaluations complete and resources released
- [ ] Processes, procedures, records, and training updated and delivered
- [ ] Project checklist complete
- [ ] Final project review and lessons learned complete
- [ ] Project documents and artifacts archived

PROJECT SUMMARY (Planned, Actual, and Comments)

Scope	
Actual	
Comments	
Schedule	
Actual	
Comments	
Budget	
Actual	
Comments	
Goal	
Actual	
Comments	
Deliverables	
Actual	
Comments	
Metrics	
Actual	
Comments	

Approvals	Approval by:	Role:	Approved date:

Regardless of your project-close and sign-off template, format, and layout, it is fundamental to include such a template in the project toolbox for final close and to secure project sign-off.

Wishing you much success in your pursuit of successfully closing projects and securing sign-off, thereby generating greater value in your organization!

Section 5:
Tool Selection and Use

One final key element of the operational excellence transformation is tool selection and use. This section of the handbook includes chapters related specifically to tools used in business today to generate value for shareholders, customers, and companies.

- 5 Why Root-Cause Analysis
- Action Plan
- Affinity Diagram
- Agenda and Minutes
- Brainstorming
- Cause-and-Effect Diagram
- Cause-and-Effect Matrix
- Control Plan
- Data Collection Plan
- Decision Tree
- Fault Tree Analysis
- Force Field Analysis
- Failure Modes and Effects Analysis (FMEA)
- Goals – SMART
- House of Quality (Quality Function Deployment)
- Impact/Effort Analysis
- Kano Analysis
- Mind Mapping
- Multivoting
- Nominal Group Technique (NGT)
- Pairwise Comparison
- Process Maps
- Pugh Matrix
- RACI
- Seven Basic Quality Tools
- SIPOC
- Six Thinking Hats
- Solution-Selection Matrix
- Status Report
- SWOT Analysis

Section 5: Tool Selection and Use

- Training Plan

Please consider these tools as essential ingredients to successful selection and use supporting the value generation journey.

5 Why

Have you ever felt that you had solved a problem only to discover it is recurring? Likely the solution was applied to a symptom of the problem, rather than the actual root cause of the problem. Asking "why" five times is a great way to find the true root cause of a problem or defect, and lead to a solution, which will prevent recurrence. Sakichi Toyoda, the founder of Toyota Industries, developed the use of 5 Why in the 1930s as part of an evolving manufacturing process.

The 5 Why root-cause analysis technique can be used as a stand-alone problem-solving tool, in combination with cause-and-effect analysis, or as part of other methodologies, such as A3 Thinking and Lean Six Sigma DMAIC.

Use 5 Why root-cause analysis when:

- Root cause in not known
- Team approach and input are preferred
- Little or no quantitative data is available
- Used as an input to a data collection plan

Benefits of using 5 Why root-cause analysis:

- Facilitate and identify root cause
- Determine root cause before solution
- Provide a collaborative team environment
- Bring together diverse backgrounds and experiences
- Save cost and time by determining and mitigating the root cause

Section 5: Tool Selection and Use

5 Why Root-Cause Analysis Process:

1. Assemble a cross-functional team of subject matter experts who will be prepared for the 5 Why root-cause brainstorming session with pre-work on the topic
2. Facilitate the brainstorming session by securing consensus for the problem or defect definition and documenting it on the root-cause analysis template
3. Ask and write down why the problem or defect occurred, why it was not detected, and why it was not prevented, using the root-cause analysis template
4. Continue to ask "why" and write down responses until the root cause(s) is/are determined
    a. The standard number of "why" questions is five, however it may take fewer or more to get to the true root cause
    b. Asking "why" may result in more than one answer, requiring branching to more than one root cause
5. Verify the root cause(s)
6. Brainstorm solutions to mitigate the root cause(s)

5 Why Root-Cause Analysis Process

Assemble team → Continue to ask why until root cause(s) is/are determined
↓
State the problem → Verify the root cause(s)
↓
Ask why the problem occurred → Mitigate the cause(s)

Root-Cause Flow-Down Example
List Problem or Defect

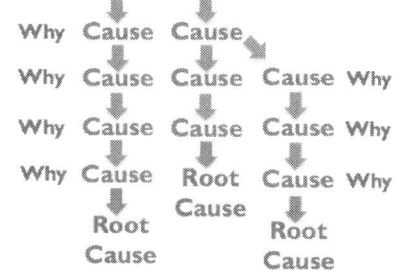

Why Cause Cause
Why Cause Cause Cause Why
Why Cause Cause Cause Why
Why Cause Root Cause Why
          Cause
Root   Root
Cause   Cause

While your root-cause analysis template may vary slightly, it will likely contain many of the components found in the following example. This image depicts a basic root-cause analysis template, along with its elements.

125

Section 5: Tool Selection and Use

Root-Cause Analysis		
Project Name:		Project Manager:
Problem or Defect Title:		
Why	Why did the Problem or Defect Occur?	Why was it not Detected?	Why was it not Prevented?
1st Why			
2nd Why			
3rd Why			
4th Why			
5th Why			

Wishing you much success in your pursuit of finding the root cause of a problem or defect, thereby generating greater value in your organization!

Action Plan

A well-executed action plan – through all phases of the project lifecycle – is essential to the success of the project. As quoted by Tom Landry, "Setting a goal is not the main thing. It is deciding how you will go about achieving it and staying with that plan." While an action plan is critical to the success of project management, it is also useful as a stand-alone tool for other endeavors in business and may be considered for any undertaking where activity assignment and ownership are necessary.

An action plan is useful when:

- A project is launched, as well as throughout the project lifecycle
- Project activities are defined by ownership with a project schedule
- The project manager and team wish to monitor progress and status of project activities

Benefits of an action plan include:

- Provide a collaborative team environment
- Save cost and time by managing project activities
- Increase focus and attention on project activities and due dates
- Provide a consistent approach for efficiently and effectively man-

Section 5: Tool Selection and Use

aging project activities

The action plan process defined below is an ideal approach for managing project activities.

Action Plan Process:

1. Define and document activities necessary to manage the project lifecycle and complete the project schedule
   a. Inputs to an action plan may include project charter, project schedule, stakeholder management plan, communication plan, resource plan, quality management plan, risk management plan, issue management plan, change control plan, training plan, and project close
2. Determine and assign ownership of the activities
3. Develop and document due dates for activities based on the project schedule
4. Monitor the status and health of activities as part of the project lifecycle and status update reports
5. Repeat the action plan process as additional activities are identified throughout the project lifecycle

Action Plan Process

- Define activities ← New
- Assign ownership
- Determine due dates
- Monitor status ←
- Status — Open / Complete
- Close action plan

An action plan may be used as an input to a lessons-learned plan or to the risk management plan. While your action plan template may vary slightly, it will likely contain many of the components found in the following example. This image depicts a basic action plan template, along with its elements.

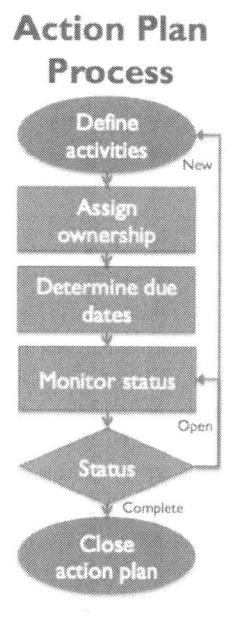

Section 5: Tool Selection and Use

	Who	What	Why	When		How	Other
#	Owner	Activity	Reason	Plan Date	Status	Approach	Comments
1							
2							
3							
4							
5							
6							
7							

Project Name: Project Manager: Action Plan

Regardless of your action plan template, format, and layout, it is fundamental to include an action plan in the project toolbox and to review it during project review meetings.

Wishing you much success in your pursuit of activity management, thereby generating greater value in your organization!

Affinity Diagram

Affinity diagram – also known as KJ Method, for Kawakita Jiro, who developed the technique in the 1960s – is a simple and powerful tool for grouping many ideas and data into natural themes.

Affinity diagrams may be used to:

- Group and understand existing data, such as
    - Voice of the customer
    - Surveys and interviews
    - Warranty and call logs
- Group and understand new data, such as brainstorming ideas on a specific topic
- Facilitate creative thinking
- Facilitate consensus

Creating an affinity diagram for new data requires facilitation skills and an understanding of brainstorming techniques.

Section 5: Tool Selection and Use

Benefits of creating an affinity diagram include:

- Provide an approach to identify and group similar ideas into logical themes
- Provide a collaborative team environment
- Bring together diverse backgrounds and experiences

Affinity Diagram Process:

1. Assemble a cross-functional team of subject matter experts who were briefed and come prepared to thoughtfully engage in the affinity session topic
2. Silently jot down on a Post-it® note or 3x5 index card – using a verb and a noun – one idea or phrase
3. Randomly post the ideas on a board or wall, with no discussion or evaluation
4. Silently read, sort, and group the ideas into common themes
    a. It may be necessary to limit the number of ideas per theme group
    b. Participants may wish to sort and group themed ideas into sub-themes
5. Define and name the themes based on the content of the ideas
6. Prioritize or vote for most important theme for further work or analysis
    a. Themes may be used for design or problem-solving efforts
    b. Themes may be used as input to additional tools, such as a data collection plan or cause-and-effect diagram

129

Section 5: Tool Selection and Use

An example of using affinity diagram is typified by a team tasked with the reduction of infection rates in a hospital operating room. The team brainstorms nearly 70 potential ideas intended to reduce infection rates. An affinity diagram is used to group the ideas into six major themes. Then, those six themes are further evaluated and defined for implementation.

Wishing you much success in your pursuit of understanding and organizing information into common themes, thereby generating greater value in your organization!

Agenda and Minutes

Agenda and minutes are foundational to successful management and governance of a project lifecycle. While agenda and minutes contribute to the success of project execution, they are very useful for all team-led endeavors in business. Paul Axtell, author of Meetings Matter, stated, "Meetings are at the heart of an effective organization, and each meeting is an opportunity to clarify issues, set new directions, sharpen focus, create alignment, and move objectives forward."

Agenda and minutes are appropriate and useful any time a group of people comes together to discuss, plan, and decide on topics and outcomes.

Benefits of an agenda and minutes include:

- Provide a collaborative team environment
- Provide an approach to document and monitor meeting assignments
- Increase focus and attention on actions and decisions resulting from meetings
- Save cost and time by adding structure and discipline to meeting management
- Provide a consistent approach for efficiently and effectively managing meeting inputs and outputs

Section 5: Tool Selection and Use

Agenda and Minutes Process:

1. Determine the meeting logistics
    a. Subject, objective, location, call-in number, date, chairperson, recorder, and invitees
    b. Inputs to an agenda may include previous minutes, project charter, project schedule, stakeholder management plan, procurement management plan, risk management plan, issue management plan, quality management plan, change control plan, data collection plan, lessons-learned plan, continuous improvement initiative, etc.
2. Determine meeting topics
    a. Responsible, start, duration, and desired results
3. Distribute the agenda in advance of the meeting to allow invitees review and preparation time
4. Conduct meeting based on agenda
    a. Chairperson manages the agenda; recorder documents the minutes
5. Distribute minutes within 24 hours of the meeting
    a. Responsible, action/decision, and due date
6. Utilize minutes for follow-up meetings and action status updates, as necessary

Agenda and minutes provide input to many other plans, activities, and undertakings during the project lifecycle. While your agenda and minutes template may vary slightly, it will likely contain many of the components found in the following example. This image depicts a basic agenda and minutes template, along with its elements.

Section 5: Tool Selection and Use

			Meeting Agenda			
Meeting Subject:						
Meeting Objective:						
Location/Call-in Number:				**Date:**		
Chair:				**Recorder:**		
Invited:						
Attended:						
#	**Responsible**	**Meeting Topic**	**Start**	**Duration**	**Desired Results**	**Comments**
1						
2						
3						
4						
5						
6						
7						

		Meeting Minutes			
#	**Responsible**	**Action/Decision**	**Due**	**Status**	**Comments**
1					
2					
3					
4					
5					
6					
7					

Wishing you much success in your pursuit of successfully managing meetings, thereby generating greater value in your organization!

Brainstorming

Brainstorming is likely the single most beneficial tool for generating powerful and useful ideas in a group or team environment. It is an efficient and effective method for generating ideas within a team by allowing participants to be creative, unbound by current paradigms. Alex F. Osborn, known as the father of brainstorming, is quoted as saying, "It is easier to tone down a wild idea than to think up a new one."

Brainstorming ground rules:

- No idea is a bad idea
- Encourage participation from all group members

Section 5: Tool Selection and Use

- Do not evaluate, criticize, or judge ideas
- Solicit quantity of ideas
- No titles in the room
- Record ideas; build on those ideas

Brainstorming may be used when:

- There is a desire to generate many ideas
- Team approach and input are preferred
- Little or no quantitative data is available
- Creative thinking and problem solving are useful

Benefits of brainstorming include:

- Provide a collaborative team environment
- Provide a consistent approach for generating ideas
- Bring together diverse backgrounds and experiences
- Provide an approach for fun, creative thinking, and new ideas
- Provide an effective and efficient approach for generating ideas

Brainstorming Process:

1. Assemble a cross-functional team of participants who are briefed and come prepared to engage in the brainstorming session
2. Open session and prepare participants by facilitating introductions and reviewing the brainstorming topic, ground rules, expectations, concerns, and deliverables of the session
3. Allow participants a few minutes in silence to think about ideas related to the brainstorming topic and session deliverables; participants will have been briefed and prepared for the topic prior to conducting the session
4. In a free-flow setting, ask participants to share their ideas with no discussion or evaluation
5. The facilitator records each idea exactly as presented on a flip chart
6. Continue presenting and recording ideas until participants have

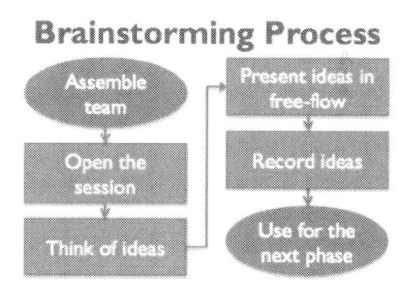

Brainstorming Process

Assemble team → Present ideas in free-flow
↓ ↑
Open the session Record ideas
↓ ↑
Think of ideas → Use for the next phase

Section 5: Tool Selection and Use

no additional ideas to add to the list or the agreed-upon time limit is reached
7. Use the brainstorming ideas for the project's next phase, such as action plan, affinity diagram, impact/effort matrix, multi-voting, Pugh matrix, solution-selection matrix, etc.

Wishing you much success in your pursuit of generating powerful and useful ideas, thereby generating greater value in your organization!

Cause-and-Effect (C&E) Diagram

A simple yet powerful tool to use in a brainstorming session to quickly generate a list of many potential causes for an effect, problem, or outcome is the cause-and-effect diagram. It's also known as a fishbone diagram for its shape, as well as the Ishikawa diagram for its inventor Kaoru Ishikawa, who developed the technique in the late 1960s.

The cause-and-effect diagram is much like an affinity diagram in that the potential causes are grouped and listed in categories or themes. One major difference is that the groups are identified first, and the brainstorming is intended to come up with ideas to list within each defined group. There are standard categories, which can be used, or the categories can be derived based on the process, problem, or effect, which the diagram represents.

There are standard cause-and-effect diagram categories common to manufacturing, service, and marketing industries, as defined in the table:

Manufacturing Industry	Service Industry	Marketing Industry
• Manpower • Mother Nature • Machines • Materials • Methods • Measurements	• Safety • Skills • Systems • Suppliers • Surroundings	• People • Price • Promotion • Place • Product • Process • Physical Evidence

Section 5: Tool Selection and Use

When to use a cause-and-effect diagram:

- There are many varying opinions for the cause
- Team approach and team input are preferred
- Little or no quantitative data is available
- As a precursor to root-cause analysis
- As an input to a data collection plan

Benefits of a cause-and-effect diagram include:

- Place cause before solution
- Facilitate root-cause analysis
- Provide a collaborative team environment
- Bring together diverse backgrounds and experiences
- Provide an approach to group causes into logical categories
- Save cost and time by determining and mitigating the true root cause

Cause-and-Effect Diagram Process:

1. Assemble a cross-functional team of subject matter experts who will be prepared for the cause-and-effect brainstorming session with pre-work on the topic
2. Facilitate the session by stating and securing consensus for the problem or effect in the form of a "why" question (Example: Why are service calls taking six or more hours per call?)
3. Determine and secure consensus for the cause categories using the standard categories or others specific to the process related to the problem or effect
4. Draw the cause-and-effect diagram, listing the problem or effect and the categories for potential causes
5. Brainstorm potential causes for each of the listed categories
6. Prioritize or vote for most important potential causes for further analysis or use as input to additional tools, such as a data collection plan or 5 Why root-cause analysis

Section 5: Tool Selection and Use

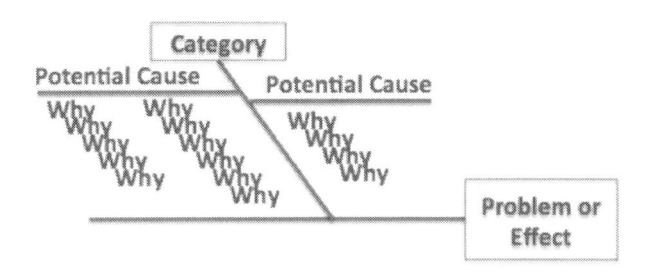

Wishing you much success in your pursuit of understanding potential causes for an effect, thereby generating greater value in your organization!

Cause-and-Effect (X-Y) Matrix

A simple yet powerful tool to use in a brainstorming session to determine a relationship between multiple causes and effects is a cause-and-effect matrix. The cause-and-effect matrix is used to determine the most important causes as related to the effects. Also known as an X-Y Matrix, it may be used to describe and understand relationships between process inputs (Xs) and process outputs (Ys).

A cause-and-effect matrix may be useful when:

- Conducting root cause analysis
- Team approach and input are preferred
- Little or no quantitative data is available
- Developing a data collection or control plan
- Defining critical process inputs relative to process outputs
- Opinions vary on the relationships between causes and effects

Benefits of a cause-and-effect matrix include:

- Provide a collaborative team environment
- Provide an approach to prioritize causes or inputs
- Save cost and time by determining critical causes or process inputs
- Bring together diverse backgrounds and experiences

Section 5: Tool Selection and Use

- Facilitate root-cause analysis, placing cause before solution

Cause-and-Effect Matrix Process:

1. Assemble a cross-functional team of subject matter experts who will be prepared for the cause-and-effect brainstorming session with prework on the topic
2. Draw the cause-and-effect matrix on the board or project an electronic cause-and-effect matrix on a screen
3. List the effects or process outputs across the top of the matrix; these may come from the SIPOC, process maps, critical-to-customer (CTC) characteristics, critical-to-quality (CTQ), or brainstorming
4. Determine the weight or importance of the effects or process outputs, and enter into the "weight" row of the matrix; weights may be determined using pairwise comparison or simply ranking on a scale of 1 to 5
5. List the causes or process inputs along the left side of the matrix; these may come from the SIPOC, process maps, cause-and-effect diagram, or brainstorming
6. Enter a relationship value of 1 for weak, 5 for medium, or 9 for strong, in the association table for each entry
7. Use the highest rank score and highest percent rank score to determine where to focus the team's activities for the next phase of the project; note that rank and percent rank scores are calculated by a formula in the matrix

Example: A manufacturer of LED flat screen televisions is working to reduce five recurring defects found during the final inspection and test process. The quality improvement team lists the five defect types as effects across the top of the matrix and the process inputs as the causes on the side of the matrix. The team gives each process input a score of 1, 5, or 9, relative to each of the defects or effects. The team then uses score results to determine process inputs that have the strongest relationships to the defects and on which to focus improvement efforts in order to reduce the defects.

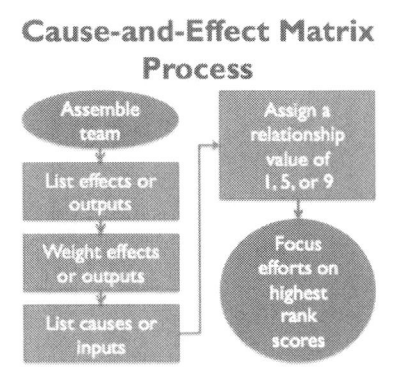

Section 5: Tool Selection and Use

While your cause-and-effect matrix template may vary slightly, it will likely contain many of the components found in the following example. This image depicts a basic cause-and-effect matrix template, along with its elements.

Wishing you much success in your pursuit of understanding causes or inputs as related to effects or outputs, thereby generating greater value in your organization!

Control Plan

A control plan is essentially a summary of the types of process controls that will be used to monitor and control critical process characteristics. It is a method for assuring that improvements will be sustained once process changes have been implemented. Process

Section 5: Tool Selection and Use

controls can also be used for any process to ensure that the process continues to perform at the desired level.

Regardless of the methodology used to manage through the project lifecycle, a control plan is a critical component to any operational excellence, continuous improvement, or transformation project. Creating and including a comprehensive control plan in the project toolbox takes careful thought and consideration by the project team to ensure critical process elements are included.

A control plan can also be a stand-alone document for ongoing process control long after the project is completed. Such a control plan should be reviewed periodically to ensure it is current and effective.

A control plan is used when:

- The project results in changes to the process, product, or service
- The project results in changes in roles and responsibilities
- A product or service includes critical characteristics
- Products or services move across changes in ownership
- Prior to a product or service reaching an irreversible point in the process

Common types of process controls include:

- Layered audits
- Process audits
- Internal audits
- Help chains
- Automated controls
- In-process inspections
- Statistical Process Control (SPC)
- Total Preventive Maintenance (TPM)

Benefits of a control plan include:

- Increase focus and attention on process control points
- Provide a consistent approach for identifying and controlling critical process input characteristics
- Provide an approach to ensure conformance to specifications and customer requirements

Section 5: Tool Selection and Use

- Save cost and time by identifying and controlling critical process input characteristics

Considerations when creating a control plan include:

- What input variables are critical to process performance?
- What process characteristics will be monitored?
- At what point in the process is it best to monitor key input characteristics?
- What are the specifications of the characteristics to be monitored?
- What type of control method will be used?
- How often is the characteristic measured and what is the sample size?
- How will the characteristic be measured?
- Who will be responsible for monitoring the characteristic and taking the measurements?
- What is the signal to indicate an out-of-control condition?
- What is the corrective action for an out-of-control condition?
- Who is responsible for the corrective action?

Control Plan Development Process:

1. Assemble a cross-functional team of subject matter experts who will be prepared for the control plan development session with pre-work on the topic
2. Review process steps and control plan inputs such as:
    a. Warranty issues
    b. Quality issues
    c. Customer complaints
    d. Lessons learned
    e. Risk and issue management plans
    f. Process maps and diagrams
    g. Failure Modes and Effects Analysis (FMEA)
    h. Cause-and-Effect Diagram
    i. Cause-and-Effect Matrix/X-Y Matrix
3. Determine the control characteristics, control points, and type of

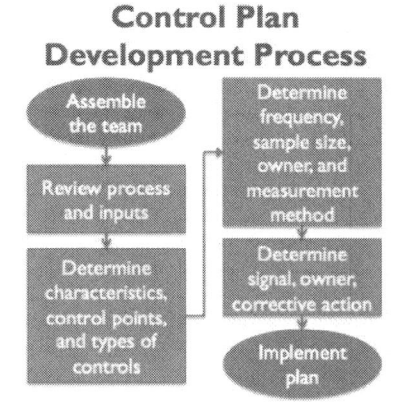

Section 5: Tool Selection and Use

control
4. Determine the frequency, sample size, responsibility, and measurement method
5. Determine the out-of-control signal, owner, and corrective action
6. Implement the control plan

While your control plan template may vary slightly, it will likely contain many of the components found in the following example. This image depicts a basic control plan template, along with its elements.

Project Name:				Project Manager:				Plan Date:		
	What			When	Who	How	What	Who	How	Other
Operation & Process Step	Characteristic	Specification & Tolerance	Type of Control	Frequency & Sample Size	Responsible	Measurement Method	Signal	Responsible	Corrective Action	Comments

Regardless of your control plan template, format, and layout, it is fundamental for larger and more complex projects to include such a plan in the project toolbox and to review it during project review meetings.

Wishing you much success in your pursuit of process control, thereby generating greater value in your organization!

Data Collection Plan

Regardless of the methodology used to manage through the project lifecycle, a data collection plan is a critical component to any operational excellence, continuous improvement, or transformation project. Creating and including a comprehensive data collection plan in the project toolbox takes careful thought and consideration by the project team to ensure time and expense are not wasted on unnecessary data collection. Sir Josiah Stamp is credited with the quote, "Public agencies are very keen on amassing statistics – they collect them, raise them to the nth power, take the cube root, and prepare wonderful diagrams. But what you must remember is that every one of the

Section 5: Tool Selection and Use

numbers comes in the first instance from the village watchman, who just puts down what he darn well pleases."

As depicted in the following image, the data collection plan ultimately drives solution sustainment through data analysis, solution selection, and implementation. There are many potential inputs used to help define the data collection plan, which include SIPOC, Process Maps, Cause-and-Effect Diagram, X-Y Matrix, Surveys, and FMEA, to name a few. To determine what data needs collected, it is important to determine the questions you wish to answer through analysis of the data.

SIPOC
Process Maps
C&E Diagram
X-Y Matrix
Surveys
FMEA

→ **Data Collection Plan** →

Graphical Analysis
Descriptive Statistics
Inferential Statistics
Root Cause Analysis
Solution Selection
Implementation
Sustainment

There are three data collection strategies to consider; they will help guide development of a data collection plan:

1. **Retrospective (Historical)** data collection is a passive strategy using data from records, systems, and files. It is typically the most accessible and the least expensive to collect. You must always be cautious using this data collection strategy, however, because you may not know how the data was originally collected or who collected it. And it may not truly represent the current process being analyzed.
2. **Observational** data collection is a passive strategy in which you or a project team member collect(s) data during the project lifecycle, while observing the process in its current state. This data collection strategy will typically result in more time and greater cost than retrospective data collection. However, it may better represent the true process in its current state. This strategy will also be necessary, if the data required has not been documented or collected in the past.
3. **Experimental** data collection is an active strategy used to find cause-and-effect relationships. This strategy provides the project team with information to optimize the process output by fine-

Section 5: Tool Selection and Use

tuning process inputs.

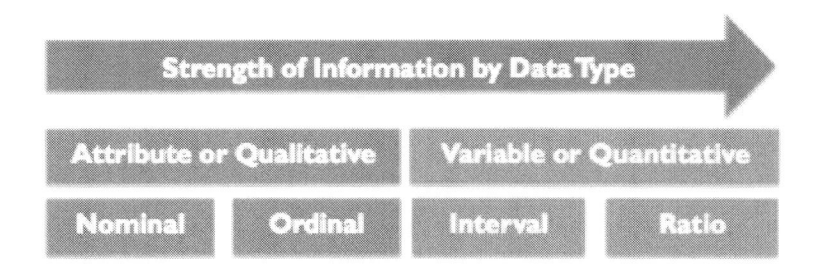

Strength of Information by Data Type

Attribute or Qualitative		Variable or Quantitative	
Nominal	Ordinal	Interval	Ratio

The four main types of data to consider for the data collection plan are nominal, ordinal, interval, and ratio. Nominal and ordinal are the least informative of the four data types. It's important to consider what questions need answered with the data analysis, which will determine what data types need collected.

1. **Nominal** (attribute or qualitative) data is defined as categories or names of information, such as colors, locations, brands, products, etc.
2. **Ordinal** (attribute or qualitative) data is non-numeric ordered categories, such as 1st, 2nd, 3rd, or strongly agree, agree, neutral, disagree, strongly disagree. While it is clear that there is an order to categories, what is not clear is the relative difference between each category.
3. **Interval** (quantitative) data is numeric data arranged in order with meaningful and exact differences – like temperature, for example. Interval data is more informative than attribute data types – because we can add or subtract temperature readings and we can calculate statistics, such as mean and standard deviation – but we cannot multiply, divide, or calculate ratios, because there is no true zero (since it is not possible to have no temperature).
4. **Ratio** (quantitative) data is the most informative of the data types. It has all of the same characteristics of interval data, plus it has a defined zero and supports many more statistical models and analyses.

Data collection requires selecting samples that are appropriate to estimate the characteristics of the population. Considerations for defining sample plans are that the data must be representative of the population, mitigate variation, and take into account all cost implications. Types of sampling plans include:

Section 5: Tool Selection and Use

- **Simple random sampling** - calculated number of random samples from a batch or group
- **Stratified random sampling** - calculated number of random samples per stratification group
- **Systematic random sampling** - taking every nth sample from a group
- **Subgroup sampling** - taking a planned number of consecutive samples during each defined time period

Before collecting the first data point, it is imperative to ensure that the measurement systems and gages are capable of providing information that represents the true process. A measurement system analysis may be conducted to validate and ensure your measurement system is capable of collecting the data defined in the plan.

Some considerations when creating a data collection plan include:

- What questions do we want to answer through data analysis?
- What are the process input variables?
- What inputs will we use to design data collection forms?
- What are the various cycles of the process?
- How can we achieve a representative sample?
- Who will collect the data?
- How will we ensure accuracy and precision in our measurement system?
- Are we using accurate operational definitions?
- What issues or barriers might we encounter?

A data collection plan is used when:

- Data is not readily available for analysis
- Root cause is not known and an analytical review is necessary
- Statistical and quantitative analysis are necessary as part of the project lifecycle

Benefits of a data collection plan include:

- Provide a consistent approach for identifying, documenting, and communicating data collection needs
- Provide a method for continuing data collection

Section 5: Tool Selection and Use

- Lead to efficient and effective data collection and analysis
- Save time and cost by prioritizing data collection needs
- Create a collaborative team culture

Data Collection Plan Process:

1. Assemble a cross-functional team of subject matter experts who will be prepared for the data collection plan development session with pre-work on the topic
2. Review inputs to the data collection plan such as:
    a. SIPOC
    b. Process maps
    c. Cause-and-effect diagram and matrix
    d. Survey
    e. FMEA
3. Determine the questions to be answered with data collection and analysis
4. Determine the operational definition of data, data type, sample size or frequency, and responsibility
5. Determine date and time, recording method, and measurement method
6. Initiate data collection; revise the plan based on analysis and learnings

Data Collection Process

- Assemble the team
- Review inputs to the plan
- Determine questions to be answered with data collection and analysis
- Determine operational definition, data type, sample, and responsibility
- Determine recording and measurement methods
- Initiate plan

A data collection plan may be used as input to a lessons-learned plan or the risk management plan. While your data collection plan template may vary slightly, it will likely contain many of the components found in the following example. This image depicts a basic data collection template, along with its elements.

Section 5: Tool Selection and Use

Data Collection Plan								
Project Name:						Project Manager:		
Who		What			When	Why	How		Other
Responsible	Operational Definition	Data Type	Sample size or Frequency	Date and Time	Questions to be Answered	Recording Method	Collection Method (Gage)	Comments

Regardless of your data collection plan template, format, and layout, it is crucial to include such a plan in the project toolbox, when data collection is necessary, and to review it during project review meetings.

Wishing you much success in your pursuit of collecting useful data, thereby generating greater value in your organization!

Decision Tree

A decision tree is a useful tool for defining, analyzing, and choosing between several alternative decisions by understanding the outcomes for each. It is a tree diagram visually displaying alternative decisions, including probability, expected value, and outcome for each. It may be used in combination with other decision-making tools, such as Pugh matrix or solution-selection matrix.

A decision tree may be useful when:

- Little quantitative data is available
- It is necessary to make a decision from among several alternatives
- Opinions vary on the best decision
- The decision will result in considerable expense and potential risks

Benefits of a decision tree include:

- Fun; easy to use and understand

Section 5: Tool Selection and Use

- Can be conducted alone or with a team; if facilitated with a team, it will
  - Bring together diverse backgrounds and experiences
  - Provide a collaborative team environment
- Support decision making when little data is available
- Provide input to additional decision-making approaches
- Ability to build in new scenarios and outcomes
- Provide an approach to analyze, challenge, and prioritize alternative decisions
- Provide an approach to determine probability, expected values, and consequences of alternative decisions

Common decision tree symbols include:

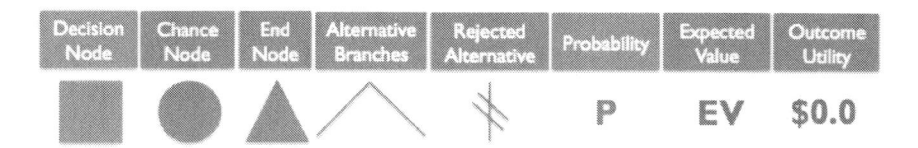

Decision Node	Chance Node	End Node	Alternative Branches	Rejected Alternative	Probability	Expected Value	Outcome Utility
■	●	▲	∧	⊬	P	EV	$0.0

Below is an example of a decision tree diagram with "Software Solution" as the subject of the decision.

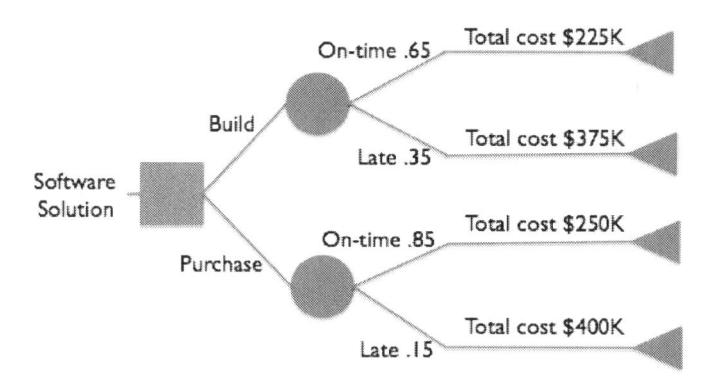

Software Solution
- Build
  - On-time .65 → Total cost $225K
  - Late .35 → Total cost $375K
- Purchase
  - On-time .85 → Total cost $250K
  - Late .15 → Total cost $400K

Decision Tree Process:

1. Define the subject for which you must make a decision
   a. Inputs to a decision tree may include goal setting, solution selection, determining a course of action, creating a strategic direction, solving a problem, etc.

Section 5: Tool Selection and Use

2. Document the subject of the decision tree on paper or flip chart, or in an electronic format
3. Add potential decisions to the decision tree subject
4. Add probability and outcome for each decision
5. Validate that all decision choices, probabilities, and outcomes have been considered and are added to the decision tree
6. Analyze the decision tree to determine the best decision choice using probabilities, outcomes, and expected values to support the final decision

Decision Tree Process

Define the subject → Add probabilities and outcomes
↓
Document the subject → Validate completeness
↓
Add potential decisions → Determine the best decision

Wishing you much success in your pursuit of examining alternatives and making an informed decision, thereby generating greater value in your organization!

Fault Tree Analysis (FTA)

Fault tree analysis is an effective tool for actual or potential failure analysis, followed by correction or prevention techniques. Originally developed in the early 1960s, fault tree analysis (FTA) was used to conduct top-down failure analysis. Primarily used in safety and reliability engineering for preventive analysis to reduce risk and prevent failure, FTA is now used in a wide range of industries and scenarios. Fault tree analysis may be conducted to determine root cause of failure as a reactive tool, or to predict preventive analysis of potential failures as a proactive tool. In either scenario, FTA starts with a single top-level event or failure, which is analyzed to determine actual or potential input faults and their root causes. An action plan to eliminate or prevent causes of input faults to the top-level failure is determined and launched as a result of the fault tree analysis.

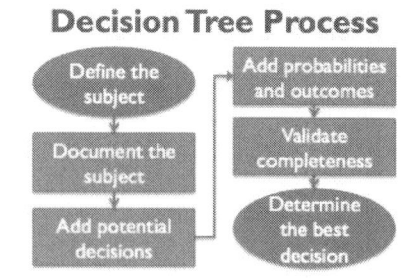

Section 5: Tool Selection and Use

The following image depicts a basic fault tree diagram example.

Fault tree top-level, input/fault, and gate example

"Or" indicates top-level failure when one or more inputs fails

"And" indicates input/fault 2 happens only when all three next level input faults happen

A fault tree analysis may be useful when:

- Quantitative data may be limited
- Opinions vary on the relationships between inputs and the top-level failure
- It is desirable to understand and correct – or prevent – causes of the top-level failure
- It is necessary and important to prioritize inputs that could lead to the top-level failure
- Failure prevention efforts take place for a system or product in the design phase

Benefits of a fault tree analysis include:

- May be conducted alone or as a team; if conducted as a team, it will
    - Bring together diverse backgrounds and experiences
    - Provide a collaborative team environment
- Facilitate reactive or preventive root-cause analysis
- Provide an approach to analyze and prioritize inputs or faults
- Identify and eliminate – or prevent – causes of the top-level failure
- Improve safety, reliability, and performance of systems and prod-

Section 5: Tool Selection and Use

ucts
- Design systems and products to prevent potential causes of the top-level failure

Common fault tree symbols include:

- Basic Event – Failure event in a process, system, or component requiring no additional analysis
- External Event – An event that is normally expected to occur
- Undeveloped Event – An event where information is not available or is determined to be unimportant
- Conditioning Event – A condition or restriction applied to a logic gate
- Intermediate Event – Used to include additional event information
- Transfer In/Out – Used to indicate a transfer to a related fault tree
- Or Gate – The event occurs if one or more of the input events occur
- And Gate – The event occurs if all of the input events occur
- Exclusive Or Gate – The event occurs if one and only one input event occurs
- Priority And Gate – The event occurs if all of the input events occur in a specific order
- Inhibit Gate – The event occurs if the input event occurs, along with a conditional input event

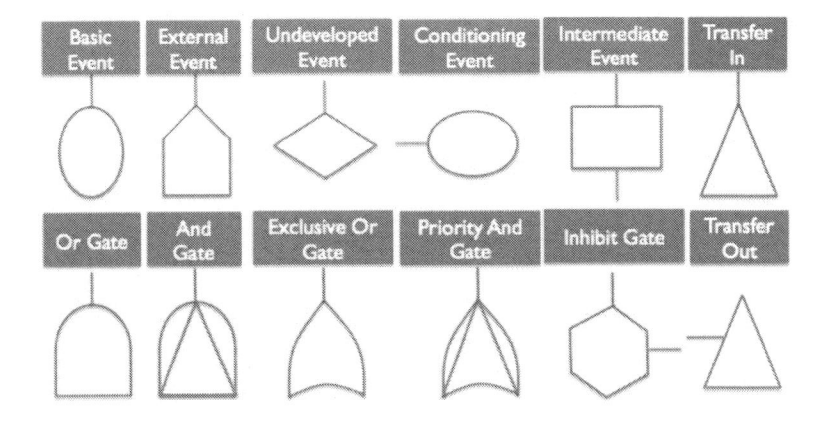

Section 5: Tool Selection and Use

Fault Tree Analysis Process:

1. Select and clearly define the top-level failure for analysis with fault tree (one top-level failure per fault tree)
    a. Inputs to a fault tree analysis may include defect records, warranty records, service logs, customer complaint logs, system performance requirements, FMEA, etc.
2. Under the top-level failure, add inputs or faults, which may or do contribute to the top-level failure
3. Under each input or fault, list all actual or potential causes of failure; if available, list the probabilities for each cause
4. Draw the fault tree diagram (top-level failure – logic gates – inputs or faults – logic gates – actual or potential causes) using the basic fault tree symbols and logic gates
5. Analyze the fault tree to determine actual or potential root cause(s) of the top-level failure
    a. Using a cause-and-effect diagram and/or 5 Why root-cause analysis at this step may be useful to determine root cause(s)
6. Define and launch
    a. Action plan (who, what, when) to correct existing root cause(s), or
    b. Risk management plan to mitigate potential risks

An example of using fault tree analysis is when an engineering team is formed to determine and prevent potential causes of car door airbags not deploying on a side impact. The team lists "car door airbags not deploying on side impact" as the top-level failure on a fault tree. They use design specifications, historical data, and crash test results to determine actual and potential input faults to the top-level failure, along with their associated causes. The information is used to create a fault tree, analyze it for root cause of the input faults, and conduct tests to validate assumptions. The team creates an action plan to implement corrections to the design to prevent actual and potential causes of the faults and top-level failure.

Section 5: Tool Selection and Use

Wishing you much success in your pursuit of understanding causes and implementing actions to correct or prevent a top-level failure, thereby generating greater value in your organization!

Force Field Analysis

Kurt Lewin's 1940s Force Field Analysis is a very powerful, yet simple, tool to evaluate opposing forces (drivers and restrainers) and to determine actions for moving toward achieving a goal or objective. Force field analysis' use has expanded over the years from its origins in social science to being used in a variety of business situations. It is a proactive approach to understand variables and forces around a particular goal or objective, and to act on the variables in a positive manner.

While a force field analysis is a powerful tool that supports achieving goals and objectives, it may be used for much more and at many levels in an organization. For example, the force field analysis supports initiatives to implement organizational change around culture, transformation, and operational excellence. Force field analysis is one of the key tools to employ in early phases of these initiatives, and it will quickly identify drivers to leverage and restrainers to mitigate.

Why do projects get delayed or sometimes fail? One possible reason for this may be because a force field analysis was not conducted, and thus restraining forces and driving forces were not understood nor managed appropriately. Consider the next time you launch a new solution, process, product, service, or even a new business. Why not use a force field analysis to understand where to focus actions and efforts?

Force field analysis may be used when:

- A strategic initiative is being evaluated for feasibility
- A new process, product, or service is being evaluated for viability
- There is concern for program or project sustainability
- A program or project is being launched or in the early phases, and to ensure success
- A new solution is being evaluated for implementation

Section 5: Tool Selection and Use

Benefits of force field analysis include:

- Proactive approach to define and mitigate restraining forces
- Provide input for developing a project plan and assigning resources
- Provide input for a communication plan and stakeholder analysis
- Provide input for directional changes for initiatives, programs, and projects
- Provide a collaborative team environment
- Bring together diverse backgrounds and experiences

Follow the steps below for a simple approach to conducting a force field analysis session:

1. Assemble a cross-functional team of subject matter experts (SMEs) who will be prepared for the session as a result of completing pre-work on the topic
2. Construct a force field analysis diagram (as follows) on a flipchart or use a template projected onto the screen
3. Validate the current situation or problem
4. List the goal or objective of the analysis
5. List the driving forces, and rank forces from 1 to 5, with 5 being the strongest
6. List the restraining forces, and rank the forces from 1 to 5, with 5 being the strongest
7. Define an action plan describing "who, what, and when" to leverage or strengthen drivers, and to mitigate or eliminate restrainers
8. Execute and manage the action plan to ensure success

Force Field Analysis Process

Assemble team → List restraining forces and rank 1 to 5 → Develop an action plan → Execute and manage the action plan

Create the diagram → List goal or objective → List driving forces and rank 1 to 5

An example of using force field analysis is a cross-functional project team tasked with implementing a new enterprise resource planning (ERP) software solution. Early in the project lifecycle, the team uses a force field analysis to understand the drivers, which would be leveraged or strengthened, and the restrainers, which must be eliminated or mitigated, to be successful with the new implementa-

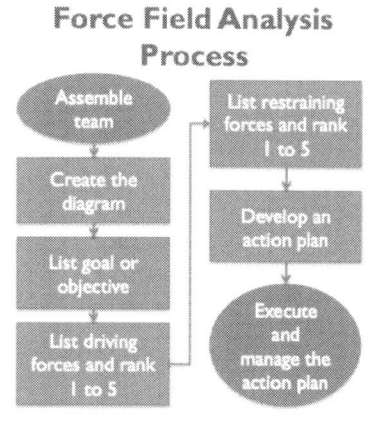

Section 5: Tool Selection and Use

tion. The information from the force field analysis helps the team define the project schedule, as well as the action plan.

A simple matrix tool, as noted in the following image, will be helpful for facilitating a force field analysis session.

VALUE GENERATION PARTNERS — Force Field Analysis			
Facilitator:		Date:	
Goal/Objective			
List Drivers	Score	List Restrainers	Score
Total Driver Score	0	Total Restrainer Score	0

Wishing you much success in your pursuit of achieving goals and objectives, thereby generating greater value in your organization!

Failure Modes and Effects Analysis (FMEA)

While the saying, "If anything can go wrong, it will," has been quoted as Murphy's Law, certainly an addendum to it could be "... and new solutions create new problems." For a new or existing product, process, or service, FMEA is an excellent approach to employ for finding and mitigating potential causes of failures. FMEA was first introduced in the late 1940s by the US Military, adopted and modified in the early 1960s by NASA, and is now widely used in most every industry.

FMEA can be used for:

- Evaluating failures or potential failures for existing services, products, or processes
- Control points for new or existing services, products, or processes
- Improvement opportunities for existing services, products, or processes

Section 5: Tool Selection and Use

- Root cause analysis for existing services, products, or processes
- An ongoing or periodic evaluation approach to preventive action and quality improvement
- Analysis of design (DFMEA) and process (PFMEA) as part of the new product or service development process

FMEA should be used when:

- The project results in a new process, product, or service
- The project impacts safety, quality, or customer service
- The project is large, complex, and costly
- New solutions will be evaluated and implemented
- Data collection and root-cause analysis will be performed

Benefits of conducting FMEA include:

- Increase focus and attention on potential failure causes
- Proactive approach for preventing the causes of potential failures from becoming failures
- Provide a consistent approach for analyzing, prioritizing, communicating, and managing potential failures
- Provide an approach to efficiently and effectively mitigate potential failures
- Provide a collaborative team environment
- Save cost and time by identifying, prioritizing, and managing potential failures

There are many sources available to find an FMEA template and to help you create your own template. And most will look similar to the images in this chapter.

Follow these listed steps for a condensed and simplified version of conducting FMEA. Your business may be subjected to specific processes or standards, potentially requiring more detail for each step.

1. Assemble a cross-functional team of subject matter experts (SMEs), who will be prepared for the session upon completing prework on the FMEA topic
2. With support of the team, complete the FMEA template as described in the following steps
3. Fill in the FMEA header

Section 5: Tool Selection and Use

VALUE	Failure Modes and Effects Analysis (FMEA)		
Item/Process:	Preparer:		Number:
Team			Date:

4. Fill in the process steps or requirements for the FMEA topic

#	Process Function (Step) (Requirements)	Potential Failure Modes (What could go wrong with process inputs, components, information, etc.)	Potential Failure Effects (The effect the failure mode has on the Output or Y variable)	S E V	Potential Causes of the Failure Mode	O C C	Current Process Controls (that could prevent or detect the Cause)	D E T	R P N
1									
2									
3									
4									
5									
6									
7									

5. List potential failure modes for each step in the process or each requirement (There may be multiple failure modes for each)
6. List potential failure effects for each failure mode
7. Rank the "severity" of each potential failure mode and effect (The ranking is typically a 1-to-10 ranking, with 10 being the most severe)

Rating	Description	Definition (Severity of Effect)
10	Dangerously high	Failure could injure the customer or an employee
9	Extremely high	Failure would create noncompliance with federal regulations
8	Very high	Failure renders the unit inoperable or unfit for use
7	High	Failure causes a high degree of customer dissatisfaction
6	Moderate	Failure results in a subsystem or partial malfunction of the product
5	Low	Failure creates enough of a performance loss to cause the customer to complain
4	Very Low	Failure can be overcome with modifications to the customer's process or product, but there is minor performance loss
3	Minor	Failure would create a minor nuisance to the customer, but the customer can overcome it without performance loss
2	Very Minor	Failure may not be readily apparent to the customer, but would have minor effects on the customer's process or product
1	None	Failure would not be noticeable to the customer and would not affect the customer's process or product

8. List potential causes for each potential failure mode
9. Rank the likelihood of "occurrence" for each potential failure mode cause (1-to-10 ranking, 10 is the most likely to occur)

Rating	Description	Definition (Likelihood of Occurrence)
10	Very High: Failure is almost inevitable	More than one occurrence per day or a probability of more than three occurrences in 10 events (Cpk < 0.33)
9	High: Failures occur almost as often as not	One occurrence every three to four days or a probability of three occurrences in 10 events (Cpk ≈ 0.33)
8	High: Repeated failures	One occurrence per week or a probability of 5 occurrences in 100 events (Cpk ≈ 0.67)
7	High: Failures occur often	One occurrence every month or one occurrence in 100 events (Cpk ≈ 0.83)
6	Moderately High: Frequent failures	One occurrence every three months or three occurrences in 1,000 events (Cpk ≈ 1.00)
5	Moderate: Occasional failures	One occurrence every six months to one year or five occurrences in 10,000 events (Cpk ≈ 1.17)
4	Moderately Low: Infrequent failures	One occurrence per year or six occurrences in 100,000 events (Cpk ≈ 1.33)
3	Low: Relatively few failures	One occurrence every one to three years or six occurrences in ten million events (Cpk ≈ 1.67)
2	Low: Failures are few and far between	One occurrence every three to five years or 2 occurrences in one billion events (Cpk ≈ 2.00)
1	Remote: Failure is unlikely	One occurrence in greater than five years or less than two occurrences in one billion events (Cpk > 2.00)

10. List current process controls for each of the potential failure mode causes
11. Rank current process controls for the "detection" ability of the potential cause or the failure mode after occurrence (1-to-10 ranking, 10 is the most uncertain to detect)

Section 5: Tool Selection and Use

Rating	Description	Definition (Ability to Detect)
10	Absolute Uncertainty	The product is not inspected or the defect caused by failure is not detectable
9	Very Remote	Product is sampled, inspected, and released based on Acceptable Quality Level (AQL) sampling plans
8	Remote	Product is accepted based on no defectives in a sample
7	Very Low	Product is 100% manually inspected in the process
6	Low	Product is 100% manually inspected using go/no-go or other mistake-proofing gauges
5	Moderate	Some Statistical Process Control (SPC) is used in process and product is final inspected off-line
4	Moderately High	SPC is used and there is immediate reaction to out-of-control conditions
3	High	An effective SPC program is in place with process capabilities (Cpk) greater than 1.33
2	Very High	All product is 100% automatically inspected
1	Almost Certain	The defect is obvious or there is 100% automatic inspection with regular calibration and preventive maintenance of the inspection equipment

12. Calculate the risk priority number (RPN) by multiplying *severity x occurrence x detection* to prioritize actions; the highest (or predetermined cut-off level) RPNs are addressed, along with any company, industry, or customer requirements with high-severity ratings
13. List recommended actions for identified RPNs and high-severity ratings
14. List the responsible person and target dates for each recommended action
15. List action taken and re-rank severity, occurrence, and detection
16. Recalculate the RPN, based on actions taken
17. Repeat the FMEA process, as necessary and as part of continuous improvement cycles

FMEA Process

Assemble the team → List process controls → List failure modes and effects → Rank detection → Rank severity → Calculate RPN → List potential causes → Take action on high priority RPNs → Rank likelihood → Recalculate the RPN

Recommend Actions	Responsible Person & Target Date	Actions Taken	S E V	O C C	D E T	R P N

Wishing you much success in your pursuit of preventive measure through FMEA, thereby generating greater value in your organization!

Section 5: Tool Selection and Use

Goals - SMART

We set goals nearly every day for many different reasons. Are our goals SMART, however? The use of SMART goals has been credited to Peter Drucker, through his management by objectives concept. The first-known writing of the term "SMART" occurs in the November 1981 issue of Management Review, in George T. Doran's article, "There's a S.M.A.R.T. Way to Write Management's Goals and Objectives."

A discussion in operational excellence and transformation would not be complete without talking about goals and, more specifically, SMART goals. While it is important to have goals – even stretch goals, when it comes to developing a goal for a transformation or improvement project, it must be SMART to succeed.

For example, suppose that you just walked out of a hospital project report-out meeting during which three projects were presented. Let's consider that the report-out format was a four-block-type review, in which the project managers presented brief overviews of their projects, accomplishments since the last review, actions for the next review, and any issues, concerns, and planned resolutions.

Now, let's consider that the three goal statements presented for the projects were:

1. Shorten Emergency Room patient wait time
2. Improve Pharmacy prescription accuracy
3. Condense patient room changeover time

What is wrong with these three goals, and how might they be better stated? In each case, we don't know current quality level, planned improvement level, and when it will be complete. While these seem like admirable goals, it is not clear that the goals are in alignment with the hospital's strategies or within the project manager's scope of influence and responsibility.

So, how could we improve these three goal statements using a SMART approach? You may have seen the SMART acronym presented in different ways – such as those displayed in the table. For this discussion, we'll use the format described in the first column,

Section 5: Tool Selection and Use

meaning that the goal is considered **SMART** if it is **S**pecific, **M**easurable, **A**chievable, **R**elevant, and **T**ime-Bound.

Specific	Specific	Specific	Strategic
Measurable	Measurable	Motivational	Measurable
Achievable	Action-Oriented	Accountable	Achievable
Relevant	Realistic	Responsible	Results-Oriented
Time-Bound	Timely	Touchable	Time-Based

To create your SMART goals, first write the goal. Then test it against the SMART goal checklist below.

1. Is the goal **S**pecific? Did you describe what process or outcome you plan to increase or decrease?
2. Is the goal **M**easurable? Did you list the current quality level and planned improvement level for when it is complete?
3. Is the goal **A**chievable? Did you base your planned quality level on facts and data?
4. Is the goal **R**elevant? Does your goal support the strategic initiatives of the organization and is it within your scope of influence and responsibility?
5. Is the goal **T**ime-Bound? Did you list a date by which to achieve the improvement level?

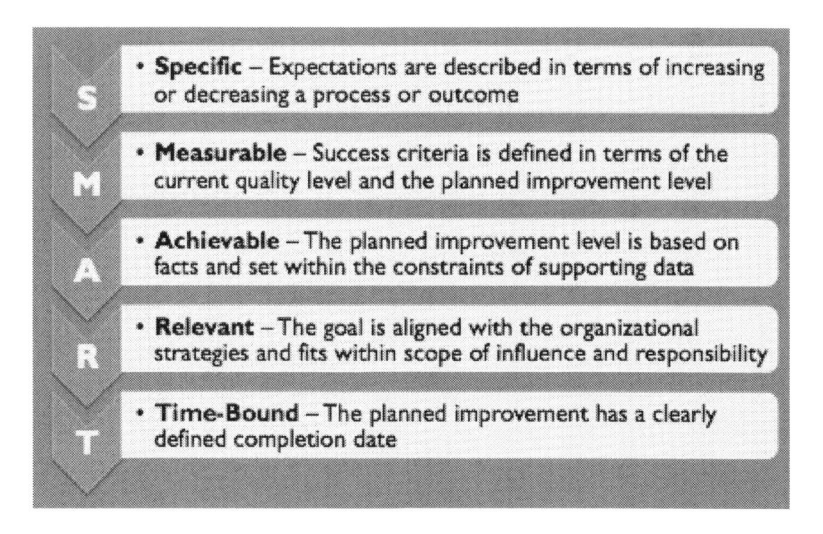

- **S** • **Specific** – Expectations are described in terms of increasing or decreasing a process or outcome
- **M** • **Measurable** – Success criteria is defined in terms of the current quality level and the planned improvement level
- **A** • **Achievable** – The planned improvement level is based on facts and set within the constraints of supporting data
- **R** • **Relevant** – The goal is aligned with the organizational strategies and fits within scope of influence and responsibility
- **T** • **Time-Bound** – The planned improvement has a clearly defined completion date

If you cannot answer "yes" to all of these SMART goal questions, continue to work on the goal until you can.

Section 5: Tool Selection and Use

Use smart goals when the project:

- Supports strategic initiatives
- Requires clarity of the deliverables
- Is time sensitive

And when the project team is:

- Measured for performance on the project results
- Rewarded based on the project results
- Responsible for delivering measurable results

Benefits of SMART goals include providing:

- Motivation to the project team
- Foundation and base for project reviews
- Clarity regarding project deliverables
- A collaborative team environment

Wishing you much success in your pursuit of achieving your objectives and goals through creating SMART goals, thereby generating greater value in your organization!

House of Quality (Quality Function Deployment)

In late 1960s, Yoji Akao and Shigeru Mizuno, both of Japan, developed Quality Function Deployment (QFD) as a method to design customer needs and requirements into new products prior to manufacture and delivery. It has since expanded into the development and delivery of services, as well. As depicted in the following image, QFD consist of four phases – or houses – starting with customer requirements and design characteristics, and managing through design of the product or service, design of the process, and design of controls. The focus of this chapter – and the first of the four phases in quality function deployment – is known as the house of quality (HOQ). House of quality translates customers' needs into design characteristics. Although QFD may include up to four phases, each with its

Section 5: Tool Selection and Use

benefits, a design team may focus much of its efforts on the first house (HOQ 1).

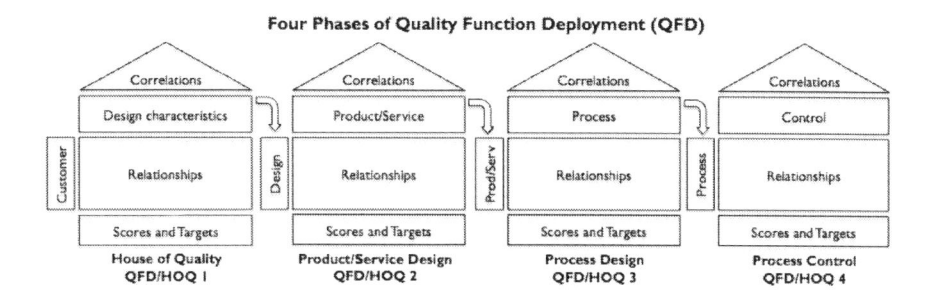

Four Phases of Quality Function Deployment (QFD)

House of Quality QFD/HOQ 1	Product/Service Design QFD/HOQ 2	Process Design QFD/HOQ 3	Process Control QFD/HOQ 4
Correlations / Design characteristics / Relationships / Scores and Targets (Customer)	Correlations / Product/Service / Relationships / Scores and Targets (Design)	Correlations / Process / Relationships / Scores and Targets (Prod/Serv)	Correlations / Control / Relationships / Scores and Targets (Process)

House of Quality consists of six (6) sections:

1. Customer requirements and priority ranking
2. Current design benchmark and competitor analysis against customer requirements
3. Design characteristics intended to deliver customer requirements
4. Strength of relationship between customer requirements and design characteristics
5. Paired correlation between each design characteristic
6. Design characteristic scores, current design benchmark and competitor analysis against design characteristics, and design targets

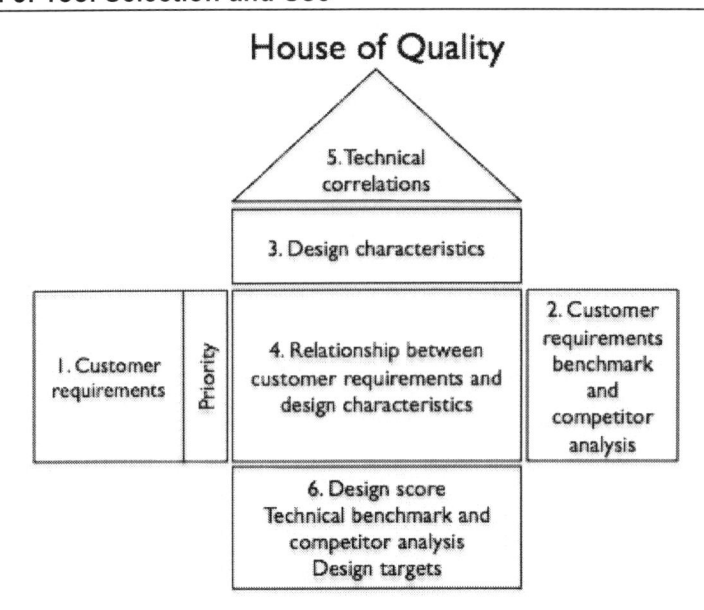

Section 5: Tool Selection and Use

House of Quality

```
                    /\
                   /  \
                  / 5. Technical \
                 /  correlations  \
                /------------------\
               |  3. Design characteristics  |
    -----------|----------------------------|----------------
   | 1. Customer | P | 4. Relationship between | 2. Customer   |
   | requirements| r | customer requirements   | requirements  |
   |             | i | and design characteristics | benchmark  |
   |             | o |                         | and           |
   |             | r |                         | competitor    |
   |             | i |                         | analysis      |
   |             | t |                         |               |
   |             | y |                         |               |
    -----------------------------------------------------------
                | 6. Design score              |
                | Technical benchmark and      |
                | competitor analysis          |
                | Design targets               |
```

House of Quality may be used when:

- Quality and competitive differentiation in product or service are desired
- The goal is to satisfy your customers, minimize costs, and maximize profitability
- There is a need to translate customer requirements into design characteristics

Benefits of House of Quality include:

- Provide a collaborative team environment
- Increase focus and attention on customer requirements and design characteristics
- Provide a consistent approach for analyzing and prioritizing customer requirements against design characteristics
- Save cost and time by identifying and prioritizing design characteristics
- Provide for shorter development and launch time at lower design and production costs
- Result in improved customer satisfaction, business results, and competitive positioning

Section 5: Tool Selection and Use

House of Quality Process:

1. Log customer requirements for the product or service based on voice of customer (VOC) data from market research, Kano model analysis, SIPOC, interviews, or other VOC methods; enter customer-provided priority level for each customer requirement based on a 1-to-5 scale (1 = not important; 5 = highest importance)
2. Enter a score of 1 to 5 (1 = did not meet; 5 = fully met) for the current design benchmark against customer requirements, and a score of 1 to 5 for the competitor designs against customer requirements
3. Enter the design characteristics identified and defined to deliver customer requirements; design characteristics are generated by project design team based on careful review and consideration of each customer requirement
4. Enter a strength of relationship value – 1 for weak, 5 for medium, or 9 for strong – for each customer requirement and design characteristic
5. Enter a paired correlation rating between each design characteristic – "+" for a strong correlation, "-" for a weak correlation, or "0" for no correlation
    a. Strong correlation indicates that increases or decreases in one design characteristic have a significant impact or relationship on the increase or decrease in another design characteristic
    b. Weak correlation indicates that increases or decreases in one design characteristic have a minimal impact or relationship on the increase or decrease in another design characteristic
    c. No correlation indicates that increases or decreases in one design characteristic have no impact or relationship on the increase or decrease in another design characteristic
6. Design characteristic priority scores are automatically calculated

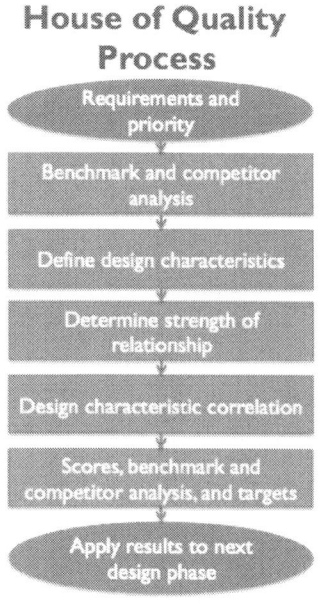

House of Quality Process

- Requirements and priority
- Benchmark and competitor analysis
- Define design characteristics
- Determine strength of relationship
- Design characteristic correlation
- Scores, benchmark and competitor analysis, and targets
- Apply results to next design phase

Section 5: Tool Selection and Use

    by the template; enter a score of 1 to 5 (1 = did not meet; 5 = fully met) for the current design benchmark against design characteristics, as well as for the competitor designs against design characteristics; enter the design specifications and targets

7. Apply the results to the next phase of product or service definition and development

While your House of Quality template may vary slightly, it will likely contain many of the elements found in the following example. This image depicts a basic House of Quality template, along with its elements.

Section 5: Tool Selection and Use

[House of Quality (QFD 1) template diagram]

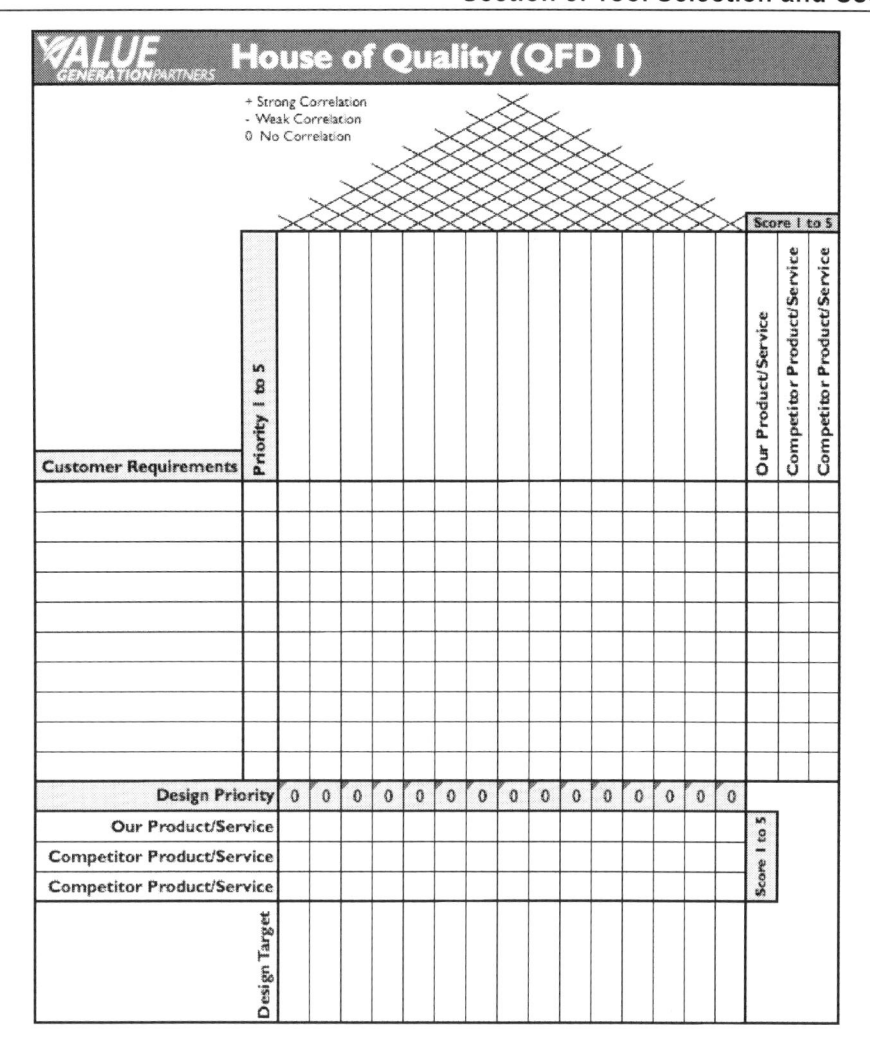

Wishing you much success in your pursuit of product or service design quality and customer satisfaction, thereby generating greater value in your organization!

Impact/Effort Analysis

An impact/effort analysis is a powerful and simple tool for prioritizing and choosing from many options. It is the process of using a matrix-

Section 5: Tool Selection and Use

style tool to evaluate several options against the impact gained and effort required for each option or idea.

Impact/effort analysis may be useful when:

- It is necessary to determine which programs, projects, problems, solutions, etc., to focus on when resources are limited
- Quantitative, objective data is not available as part of the evaluation, selection, and decision-making process
- A choice must be made from several options, and it is necessary to screen the options relative to impact gained and effort required

Benefits of impact/effort analysis include:

- Provide a consistent and efficient approach for prioritizing and choosing from many options
- Reduce emotion and bias from the decision-making and prioritization process
- Provide a collaborative team environment
- Results of many options are displayed on one matrix-style tool

Impact/Effort Analysis Process:

1. Assemble a cross-functional team of subject matter experts (SMEs) who will be prepared for the session as a result of completing pre-work on the topic
2. Brainstorm a list of potential options for evaluation based on the impact/effort topic or use a prepared list from a previous brainstorming session
3. Construct an impact/effort matrix on a flipchart or use a template projected onto the screen
4. Evaluate each option for impact gained and effort required, and place the option number or identification in the appropriate impact/effort cell on the matrix
5. Select and focus on the options with the highest impact at the lowest possible effort

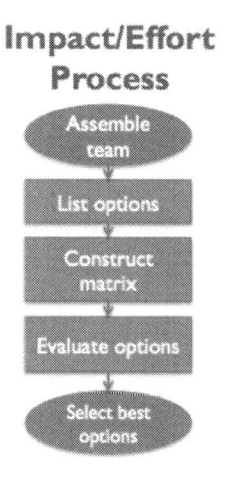

Impact/Effort Process

- Assemble team
- List options
- Construct matrix
- Evaluate options
- Select best options

Section 5: Tool Selection and Use

VALUE GENERATION PARTNERS Impact/Effort Matrix

Project Name:		
Project Manager:		Date:

Impact (High / Medium / Low) vs Effort (Low / Medium / High)

An example of using an impact/effort matrix is by an improvement team working together to determine which of many options are best suited to reduce emergency room wait times. The team evaluates each option for impact (how much it would reduce the emergency room wait time) and effort (how difficult and costly it will be to implement). The options with the highest impact and lowest effort are chosen to implement.

Impact/effort analysis is a powerful approach for prioritizing and choosing from multiple options.

While the matrix tool is described using impact and effort as evaluation categories, the same matrix – and approach – may be used to evaluate options against other categories, such as cost/benefit, impact/risk, value/effort, etc. The matrix indicates that the options are evaluated from a low, medium, and high perspective, yet the criteria may be replaced with elements based on specific and organizational needs. For example: Low, medium, and high may be replaced with appropriate dollar values, if the matrix would be used to do a cost/benefit analysis, rather than an impact/effort. As you can see, the matrix categories and criteria may be tailored to your organizational needs.

Section 5: Tool Selection and Use

Wishing you much success in your pursuit of prioritizing many options relative to impact and effort, thereby generating greater value in your organization!

Kano Model Analysis

Developed in the 1980s by Professor Noriaki Kano, Kano model analysis is a customer satisfaction and development tool. The Kano model classifies customer preferences into five categories. Kano model analysis is a powerful and useful approach for determining characteristics to include in a new product or service. When a Kano analysis is conducted and its outcomes are applied, it will result in a profitable and competitive differentiator, where customers become excited about and loyal to your business. Wal-Mart's founder Sam Walton said, "Exceed your customers' expectations. If you do, they'll come back over and over. Give them what they want – and a little more."

How Kano helps define customer needs:

- **Must haves** – expected characteristics of a product or service that must be present to allow entry into a market; without these, the customer will go to another source
- **Core requirements** – desired characteristics of a product or service that allow you to remain in a market; these characteristics improve customer satisfaction level
- **Exciters** – unexpected characteristics of a product or service that a customer does not expect; these differentiate you in the market

Kano model analysis is used when:

- Voice-of-customer (VOC) needs are reviewed to determine characteristics of a new product or service
- Competitive differentiation in product or service characteristics is desired
- The goal is to delight your customers and maximize profitability with a competitive advantage

Section 5: Tool Selection and Use

Benefits of a Kano model analysis include:

- Increase focus and attention on delighting customers
- Provide a consistent approach for analyzing and prioritizing product or service characteristics
- Save cost and time by identifying and prioritizing product or service characteristics
- Provide an approach for efficiently and effectively differentiating a product or service

Kano Model Analysis Process:

1. Aggregate voice-of-customer needs by conducting interviews, surveys, and focus groups, and reviewing customer complaints, warranty data, etc.
2. Based on aggregation of voice-of-customer data, create a list of potential customer-needed characteristics for the product or service

Kano Model Analysis Process

3. Obtain feedback through interviews or surveys to determine how customers will feel if a potential need is or is not addressed
    - The positive question format is, "How would you feel if the need is addressed?"
    - The negative question format is, "How would you feel if the need is not addressed?"
    - The customer can respond with one of four choices for positive and negative question formats
        a. I like it
        b. It's normal
        c. I don't care
        d. I don't like it
4. Summarize the customer feedback and categorize potential needs into one of five requirement categories:
    - **Must haves** – or **dissatisfiers** – are **expected** characteristics of a product or service that do not increase satisfaction, yet dissatisfy if not present; examples may include on-time airline flight schedules, restaurant cleanliness, accurate billing statements

Section 5: Tool Selection and Use

- **Core requirements** – or **satisfiers** – are **desired** characteristics of a product or service that increase or decrease satisfaction based on amount or degree; examples may include delivery time, price, ease of use
- **Exciters** – or **delighters** – are **unexpected** characteristics that impress the customer and differentiate the product or service; examples may include complimentary in-flight Wi-Fi, 75 miles per gallon fuel economy, complimentary car wash with every oil change
- **Indifferent** – customer does not care if the characteristic is present or not present; thus, do not spend time or resources on these characteristics
- **Reverse** – characteristic that causes customer dissatisfaction; thus, do not include these characteristics in the final product or service

Customer Need	Negative			
	Like it	Normal	Don't Care	Don't Like it
Positive Like it		Exciter	Exciter	Core
Normal	Reverse	Indifferent	Indifferent	Must Have
Don't Care	Reverse	Indifferent	Indifferent	Must Have
Don't Like it	Reverse	Reverse	Indifferent	

5. Create a Kano model diagram by plotting characteristics based on three categories:
    - **Must-haves** curve suggests that satisfaction does not increase if the characteristic is present; however, satisfaction decreases if the characteristic is not present
    - **Core requirements** line suggests that satisfaction increases or decreases proportionately to the presence of the characteristic
    - **Exciters** curve suggests that satisfaction increases if the characteristic is present; however, satisfaction does not decrease if the characteristic is not present

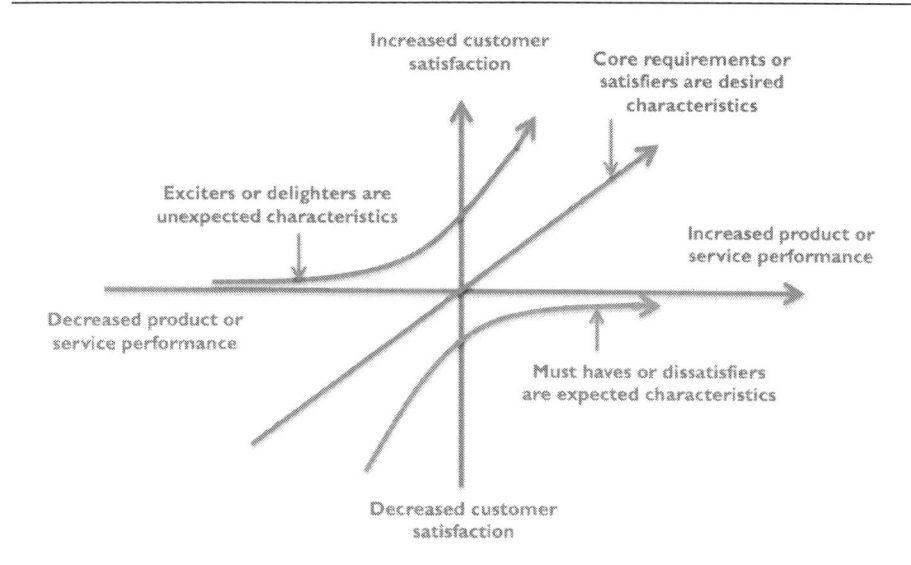

Section 5: Tool Selection and Use

[Kano model diagram showing axes of customer satisfaction vs. product/service performance, with curves for Exciters/delighters (unexpected characteristics), Core requirements/satisfiers (desired characteristics), and Must haves/dissatisfiers (expected characteristics).]

6. Apply results of Kano model to next phase of product or service definition and development

Wishing you much success in your pursuit of delighting your customers, thereby generating greater value in your organization!

Mind Mapping

Mind mapping is a powerful, simple tool to use in a brainstorming session to visually represent and analyze ideas. It is a pictorial-style thinking approach, which focuses on one central topic and allows information to be structurally portrayed for analysis and prioritization.

Unlike lists of ideas generated from typical brainstorming approaches, ideas generated through mind mapping connect to a single central topic in a branch-like diagram. Each new idea may generate an additional branch connected directly to the central topic, or expanded as a sub-idea from an existing main idea.

Mind mapping may be useful when:

- Little or no quantitative data is available

Section 5: Tool Selection and Use

- Creative thinking and problem solving are useful
- A team approach and input are preferred
- Organizing and presenting information in a visual method are desired

Benefits of mind mapping include:

- Bring together diverse backgrounds and experiences
- Provide an approach for generating creative thoughts and ideas
- Provide an approach for pictorial presentation of ideas
- Provide a collaborative team environment

Mind Mapping Process:

1. Assemble a team of participants who were briefed and come prepared to engage in the mind mapping central topic
2. Write the central topic on a board or flip chart
3. Brainstorm, write, and connect main ideas related to the central topic on the board
4. Brainstorm, write, and connect sub-ideas related to the main ideas on the board
5. Continue to brainstorm ideas until no additions are necessary
6. Use mind map for next phase of the project or initiative, such as an action plan or prioritization process

Mind Mapping Process

- Assemble the team
- Write central topic on board
- Connect main ideas to central topic
- Connect sub-ideas to main ideas
- Use for the next phase

Section 5: Tool Selection and Use

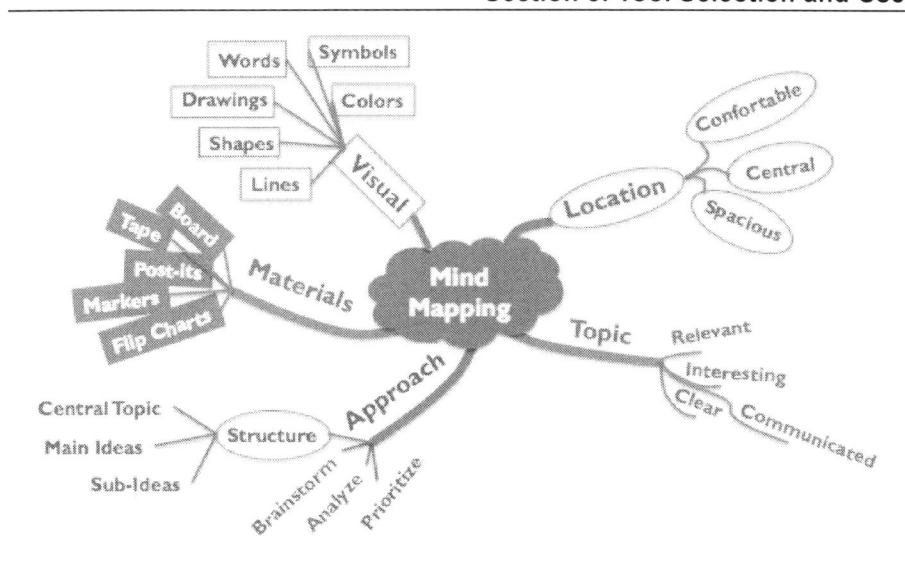

Mind mapping examples:

Central Topic Examples	Potential Main Ideas to Connect to the Central Topic
Plan a Vacation	Destinations, Timing, Length of Stay, Method of Transportation
Plan a Meeting	Location, Duration, Attendees, Agenda
Landscape Yard	Size, Location, Flowers, Shrubbery
Design a Smart Phone	Size, Features, Functionality, Colors, Materials, Manufacturer
Open a Restaurant	Location, Menu, Service Type, Seating Style

The central topics listed in the examples above will be written at the center of the mind map, and the main ideas listed become branches. Participants continue to brainstorm potential main ideas to connect to the central topic and sub-ideas to connect to the main ideas. Once the mind map is complete, participants will evaluate the ideas for relevancy, priority, and next steps.

Wishing you much success in your pursuit of creative visualization, understanding, and analysis of a key topic, thereby generating greater value in your organization!

173

Section 5: Tool Selection and Use

Multivoting

Multivoting is a simple, efficient approach for selecting and reaching group consensus on the most important ideas from a list on which to focus. It can be thought of as reducing the trivial many to the critical few.

Multivoting may be used when:

- There are too many ideas on which to focus
- Consensus for selecting ideas is preferred
- Team approach and input are preferred
- Opinions vary on which ideas should take priority

Benefits of multivoting include:

- Provide a collaborative team environment
- Provide a consistent approach for selecting ideas
- Provide an effective and efficient approach for selecting ideas
- Facilitate building consensus
- Save time and cost by focusing on select ideas

Multivoting Process:

1. Assemble a team prepared to conduct multivoting session on an existing list of ideas or by brainstorming a new list of ideas
2. Write each idea on a flip chart and assign consecutive numbers, starting with one (1) through the entire list of ideas
3. Provide each participant with a limited number of colored dot stickers (usually one-third of the total number of ideas listed)
4. Ask participants to vote on their choice for the top ideas by placing a dot next to an idea
    a. Determine the maximum number of votes each participant may post on a single idea
    b. If appropriate, voting may be done in confidence by asking

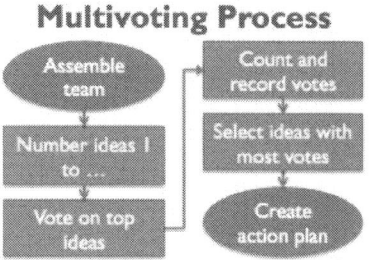

Multivoting Process

Assemble team → Number ideas 1 to ... → Vote on top ideas → Count and record votes → Select ideas with most votes → Create action plan

174

Section 5: Tool Selection and Use

   participants to write on a piece of paper their votes for top choices
5. Record the total number of votes for each idea
   a. If necessary, repeat the multivoting process on the ideas with the highest votes until the list of ideas with the most votes is manageable for taking action
6. Develop an action plan (who, what, and when) for ideas with the most votes

An example of using multivoting is characterized by a team challenged with determining select ideas, from a list of 20, on which to focus their efforts. A list of brainstorming ideas is developed by the team to reduce customer wait time at a service desk for issuing license plates and car titles in a government office. The team decides to use multivoting to select the top five ideas from the list. Using a cut-off value of five votes after the first round of voting, there are eight ideas remaining on the list. With limited resources and time, the team wishes to reduce the list to five ideas. The team conducts a second round of multivoting on the remaining list of eight ideas; it becomes clear by the number of votes those top five ideas the team feels is most important to implement. There is full support and ownership by the team and sponsor to proceed with implementation of the ideas numbered 2, 5, 6, 10, and 17. See the voting table image for the votes cast in two rounds.

Idea No.	1st Vote Score	New List	2nd Vote Score	Final List
1	0			
2	10	2	7	2
3	0			
4	7	4	0	
5	9	5	6	5
6	6	6	5	6
7	0			
8	6	8	0	
9	0			
10	7	10	6	10
11	0			
12	4			
13	5	13	2	
14	0			
15	3			
16	0			
17	8	17	6	17
18	0			
19	3			
20	2			

Wishing you much success in your pursuit of identifying the critical-few ideas on which to prioritize and focus, thereby generating greater value in your organization!

Section 5: Tool Selection and Use

Nominal Group Technique (NGT)

Nominal group technique (NGT) is an effective approach to generate, clarify, and prioritize ideas. It is a combination of brainstorming and multivoting, with a twist on the idea-generation component of the process. It provides an approach to include all participants in the discussion process, thus avoiding concerns, conflict, and criticism.

Nominal group technique ground rules:

- No idea is a bad idea
- Encourage participation from all
- Do not criticize or evaluate ideas
- Solicit quantity of ideas
- No titles in the room
- Record ideas; build on those ideas

Nominal group technique may be used when:

- Strength of personalities vary within the group of participants
- Levels of authority vary within the group of participants
- There is reluctance to participate by some participants
- There are new members to the group
- Topic of the session may be perceived by some as controversial in nature
- Generating a quantity of ideas is difficult

Benefits of nominal group technique include:

- Provide an approach for equal participation
- Provide a safe, fair environment for participants
- Bring together diverse backgrounds and experiences
- Provide a collaborative team environment
- Provide an effective and efficient approach for generating, clarifying, and prioritizing ideas

Section 5: Tool Selection and Use

Nominal Group Technique Process:

1. Assemble a cross-functional team of participants who are briefed and come prepared to engage in the brainstorming session
2. Prepare the session participants by facilitating introductions and reviewing the brainstorming topic, ground rules, expectations, concerns, deliverables of the session

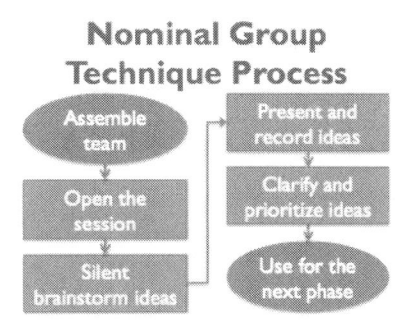

Nominal Group Technique Process

Assemble team → Present and record ideas
↓ ↓
Open the session → Clarify and prioritize ideas
↓ ↓
Silent brainstorm ideas → Use for the next phase

3. Allow participants five to ten minutes in silence to generate ideas related to the session topic and deliverables; participants will have been briefed on and prepared for the topic prior to the session
4. In a round robin arrangement, ask each participant to verbally state one idea at a time with no discussion or evaluation; facilitator records each idea on a flip chart exactly as presented; continue presenting and recording ideas until participants have no more ideas to add to the list or the agreed-upon time limit is reached
5. Review and clarify each idea on the list, seeking approval by idea contributor; reword, where necessary; with agreement by participants, strike an idea from the list
6. Prioritize the ideas using impact/effort matrix, multivoting, pairwise comparison, selection matrix, etc.
7. Use these prioritized ideas for the next phase of the project or initiative, such as an action plan

Wishing you much success in your pursuit of generating, clarifying, and prioritizing powerful and useful ideas, thereby generating greater value in your organization!

Pairwise Comparison

Pairwise comparison (also known as paired comparison) is a powerful and simple tool for prioritizing and ranking multiple options relative

Section 5: Tool Selection and Use

to each other. It is the process of using a matrix-style tool to compare each option in pairs and determine which is the preferred choice or has the highest level of importance based on defined criteria. At the end of the comparison process, each option has a rank or relative rating as compared to the rest of the options.

Pairwise comparison may be useful when:

- Quantitative, objective data is not available as part of the evaluation and decision-making process
- It is necessary to determine which programs, projects, problems, etc., to focus on when resources are limited
- A choice must be made from several options, and it is necessary to screen the options relative to each other
- Decision or selection criteria must be weighted or ranked for importance relative to each other prior to using in a decision or selection matrix

Benefits of pairwise comparison include:

- Provide a consistent and efficient approach for prioritizing or ranking multiple options
- Provide a collaborative team environment
- Reduce emotion and bias from the decision-making process

Pairwise Comparison Process:

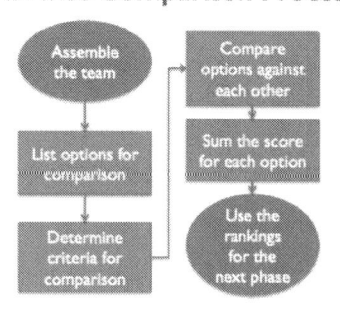

1. Assemble a team of stakeholders who are vested in the pairwise comparison options and topic
2. List the options for comparison along the "X" and "Y" axes of the Pairwise Comparison Matrix
   a. In the image, notice that each option is assigned a letter to represent the option in the comparison matrix
3. Determine the criteria for comparison, such as which option is preferred in terms of cost, customer impact, financial impact, resource requirements, risk level, etc.

Pairwise Comparison Process

Assemble the team → Compare options against each other

List options for comparison → Sum the score for each option

Determine criteria for comparison → Use the rankings for the next phase

178

Section 5: Tool Selection and Use

4. Compare each option in the rows to each option in the columns, and place the letter of the preferred or most important option in the cell, which aligns the two options
    a. Notice that the matrix does not allow options to be compared to themselves, or to each other more than one time
5. Once all options are compared, sum the number of times each letter appears in the matrix for the prioritization ranking of each option; note that the matrix template performs the calculation
    a. If necessary or useful, convert the rankings to percentages
6. Use the prioritization ranking of the options for the next phase of the decision-making process

An example of using pairwise comparison is a project team working with the sponsor to prioritize seven project deliverables. The team lists the project deliverables from "A" to "G" on both axes of the pairwise comparison matrix. Using the matrix, each deliverable is compared in pairs. (Example: Compare deliverable A to deliverable B, then deliverable A to deliverable C, etc.) During the comparison process, the sponsor determines which is the most important deliverable in the pair, and its letter is placed in the corresponding cell. At the end of the comparison, the deliverables are ranked for priority by the number of times a deliverable's representative letter is used.

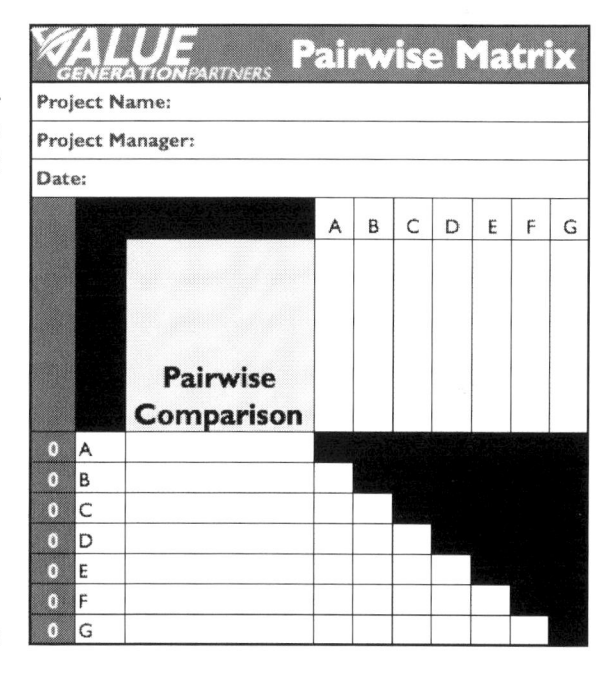

Pairwise comparison is a powerful tool for ranking and prioritizing multiple options.

179

Section 5: Tool Selection and Use

Wishing you much success in your pursuit of prioritizing or ranking multiple options relative to each other, thereby generating greater value in your organization!

Process Maps

W. Edwards Deming is credited with the phrase, "If you can't describe what you are doing as a process, you don't know what you're doing." A process can be defined as any activity or group of activities that transforms inputs by adding value and providing an output to an internal or external customer. Process maps are the tools used to visually describe what you are doing and how you are doing it.

Inputs	Transformation	Outputs
People Equipment Environment Procedures Materials	Process	Product or Service

Process maps are made up of the following elements:

- **Inputs** are variables that contribute to or influence a process step
- **Controllable Inputs** are variables that can easily be changed to measure the effect on an output
- **Critical Inputs** are variables that have been statistically proven to effect one or more of the outputs
- **Noise Input** are variables that are very difficult to control
- **Value Added (VA)** is a process step that transforms the product or service in a way that adds value to the customer
- **Non-Value Added (NVA)** is a process step that does not transform the product or service in a way that adds value to the customer
- **Non-Value Added but Necessary (NVAN)** is a process step that does not transform the product or service in a way that adds value to the customer, but is required, typically, due to regulatory compliance

Section 5: Tool Selection and Use

- **Outputs** are variables that result from a particular process step

As you reflect on the elements of a process, it is important to consider that all inputs have variation, all processes include value-added and non-value-added activities, and the outputs are the sum of the variation, value-added, and non-value-added activities. A well-defined and documented process map provides a starting point for future work on the process to reduce variation and eliminate non-value-added activities.

When conducting a process-mapping session, it is advantageous to encourage team members to follow (or walk) the process. The team must then come to consensus on the process steps as the final version of the map is documented. Process maps are living documents that get updated as the process changes or improvements are implemented.

Depending on the process, there are many types of process maps from which to choose to document the steps, such as the three listed below:

1. Flowcharts and block diagrams
2. Input/output process map
3. Deployment flowcharts or swimlane maps

Below are some basic and typical symbols to use when creating flowcharts and process maps:

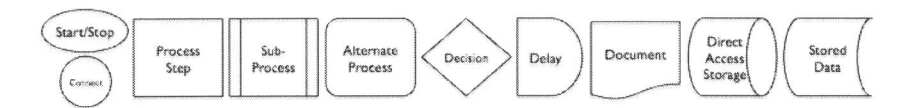

![Flowchart symbols: Start/Stop, Connect, Process Step, Sub-Process, Alternate Process, Decision, Delay, Document, Direct Access Storage, Stored Data]

Flowcharts and block diagrams are typically used to depict simple processes with few steps. Flowcharts may be used to document process flows that do not cross multiple functions or do not require an understanding of the inputs and outputs. They may be used as a high-level view of the process or a starting point for more detailed process maps.

181

Section 5: Tool Selection and Use

Flowchart or Block Diagram

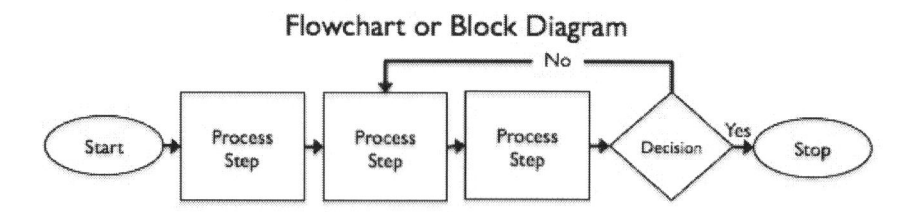

Benefits of flowcharts and block diagrams include:

- Provide a staring point for more detailed mapping
- Provide a simple and high-level visual depiction of the process flow
- Provide a consistent approach for analyzing and improving simple process flows

Process for documenting flowcharts and block diagrams:

1. Assemble a cross-functional team of subject matter experts on the process to be documented
2. Identify and document the starting point and stopping point; these are the boundaries of the process
3. Document the process steps, including any decision points, delays, documentation, etc.
4. Utilize the flowchart for the next phase of the initiative, such as to document procedures, conduct process training, or for process improvement

Input/output process maps are used to describe and understand processes with multiple steps that transform materials, services, or information into customer deliverables. These maps focus on understanding each process step, along with its associated inputs and outputs. Input/output process maps are typically used to find, understand, and correct sources of variation and to ensure the final output meets customer specifications.

Section 5: Tool Selection and Use

Input/Output Process Map

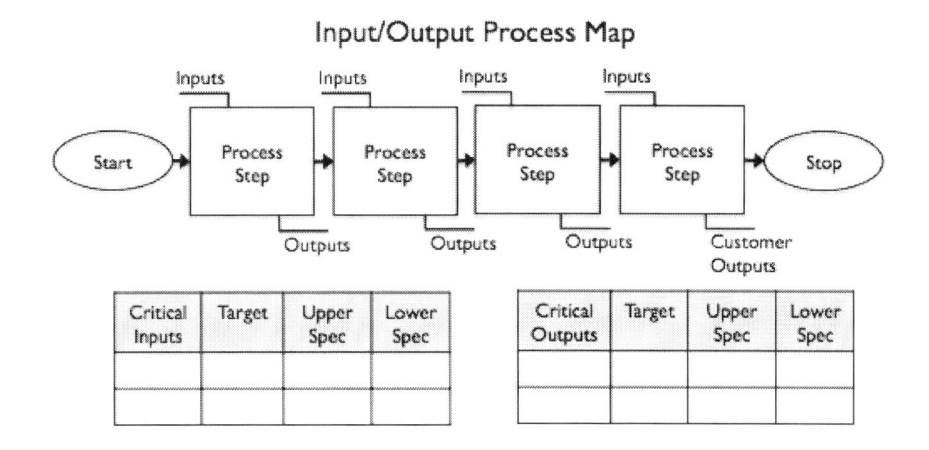

```
Inputs      Inputs      Inputs      Inputs
  ↓           ↓           ↓           ↓
Start → Process → Process → Process → Process → Stop
        Step       Step      Step      Step
          ↓          ↓         ↓         ↓
       Outputs   Outputs   Outputs   Customer
                                     Outputs
```

Critical Inputs	Target	Upper Spec	Lower Spec

Critical Outputs	Target	Upper Spec	Lower Spec

Benefits of input/output process maps:

- Provide a view of potential control points
- Provide a starting point for more detailed mapping
- Provide a high-level or detailed visual depiction of the process flow
- Provide a consistent approach for analyzing and improving process flows
- Provide a view of delays, decision points, non-value-added activities, and areas of variation

Process for documenting input/output process maps:

1. Assemble a cross-functional team of subject matter experts on the process to be documented
2. Identify and document the starting point and stopping point; these are the boundaries of the process
3. Document the key process steps, including any decision points, delays, documentation, etc.
4. Document inputs for each process step
5. Document outputs for each process step
6. Identify critical outputs for each process step and customer
7. Identify critical inputs for each process step
8. Add targets and operating specification for critical inputs and outputs
9. Utilize the process map for the next phase of the initiative, such as to document procedures, conduct process training, or for pro-

Section 5: Tool Selection and Use

cess improvement

Deployment flowcharts or swimlane maps are used to understand and depict processes in situations when information, materials, and services flow with handoffs across multiple functions. These maps are typically used to find, understand, and correct sources of non-value-added waste in transactional or business processes. Creating a deployment flowchart, it becomes clear where there are handoffs, decision points, delays, loop backs, and redundant process steps.

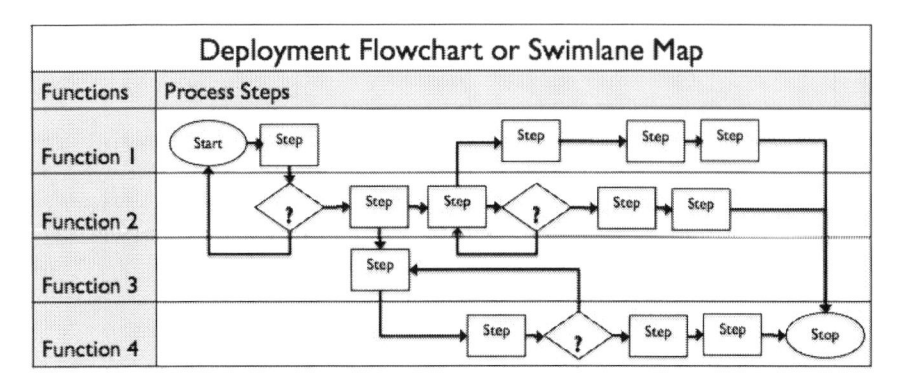

Deployment Flowchart or Swimlane Map	
Functions	Process Steps
Function 1	Start → Step → Step → Step → Step
Function 2	? → Step → Step → ? → Step → Step
Function 3	Step
Function 4	Step → ? → Step → Step → Stop

Benefits of deployment flowcharts or swimlane process maps:

- Provide a starting point for more detailed mapping
- Provide a high-level or detailed visual depiction of transactional or business processes
- Provide a consistent approach for analyzing, transactional, or business process flows
- Provide a view of non-value-added activities, such as handoffs, decision points, delays, loop backs, and redundant process steps

Process for documenting deployment flowcharts or swimlane process maps:

1. Assemble a cross-functional team of subject matter experts on the process to be documented
2. Identify and document the starting point and stopping point; they are the boundaries of the process
3. Define and document the key function or department names for each swimlane represented by the process
4. Document the flow as process steps, handoffs, decision points,

Section 5: Tool Selection and Use

and loop backs through various swimlanes
5. Utilize the process map for the next phase of the initiative, such as to document procedures, conduct process training, or for process improvement

Any of the referenced flow charts and process maps may be used as inputs to other tools and efforts, such as:

- Cause-and-effect diagram
- Cause-and-effect matrix
- Data collection plan
- Risk management plan
- Training plan
- Control plan
- Work instructions or procedures
- Improvement projects and initiatives

Wishing you much success in your pursuit of understanding and documenting your processes, thereby generating greater value in your organization!

Pugh Matrix

A Pugh matrix is a selection tool used to help choose between multiple concepts for a new process, product, or service. It was originally used to evaluate and select between several product or process designs, as ranked against customer criteria and the current baseline design. Pugh matrix, also known as Pugh method and Pugh concept selection, was developed by Stuart Pugh and published in Total Design in 1991. While a Pugh matrix is typically used to select the best alternative among product or process designs, it may also be used to define a hybrid solution, using the best characteristics from several alternative concepts. Pugh may also be used as an alternative to the solution-selection matrix for choosing the best solution for a problem-solving project.

A Pugh matrix may be used when:

- The current process, product, or service requires redesign or im-

Section 5: Tool Selection and Use

provement
- The current design is not meeting customer requirements or performing as required
- Choosing the best concept or a combination of the best characteristics among several concepts

Benefits of a Pugh matrix include:

- Reduce emotion and bias from the decision-making process
- Provide a consistent approach for selecting among several concepts
- Provide a tool to define a hybrid design or solution based on the best characteristics from several options
- Save cost and time by efficiently and effectively selecting the best design for a new process, product, or service

Pugh Matrix Process:

1. Assemble a cross-functional team of subject matter experts who will be prepared for the Pugh matrix session with pre-work on the topic
2. Draw a Pugh matrix on a board or flipchart, or project an electronic matrix on a screen
3. Enter into the matrix the current design as the baseline for comparative ranking among the concepts

Pugh Matrix Process

Assemble the team → Determine criterion weight → Enter current baseline design → Rank concepts (+1, 0, -1) → List optional concepts → Sum the scores for each concept → List key design criterion → Select best concept

4. List or brainstorm optional concept designs determined to meet the voice-of-the-customer and voice-of-the-business needs for a new process, product, or service
5. List or brainstorm key criteria from which to evaluate concept options; key criteria may include critical-to-customer, critical-to-business, critical-to-quality, and critical design characteristics
6. Determine a weighting factor for each of the key criteria; weights may be determined using pairwise comparison or simply ranking on a scale of 1 to 5
7. Evaluate each concept against the current baseline design for each criterion and provide a score of +1 for better than, 0 for

Section 5: Tool Selection and Use

      same as, or -1 for worse than the current baseline design
8. Sum the positive, negative, and total scores for each concept; note that the matrix template performs the calculations
9. Determine the weighted total score by multiplying each criterion weight times the individual concept score, then summing the total for each concept; note that the matrix template performs the calculations
10. Use the highest (positive) scores to determine which design concept or combination of design criterion characteristics from each concept to carry forward to the next phase of the decision or development process

An example of using a Pugh matrix is when a design team is tasked to develop a next generation smart phone. The team lists the current smart phone design as the baseline, and brainstorms four new design concepts to include in the evaluation matrix. The key design characteristics are listed in the matrix as the evaluation criterion, and each of the four design concepts are evaluated against the baseline to determine if the concept is better than, equal to, or worse than the baseline for each criterion. The concept with the best (highest, positive) score, as measured against the baseline, is used for the next design phase of the new smart phone.

While your Pugh matrix template may vary slightly, it will likely contain many of the components found in the following example. This image depicts a basic Pugh matrix template, along with its elements.

Section 5: Tool Selection and Use

	Baseline	Concept 1	Concept 2	Concept 3	Concept 4	Weight
Key Criteria						
Criterion 1	0					
Criterion 2	0					
Criterion 3	0					
Criterion 4	0					
Criterion 5	0					
Criterion 6	0					
Sum of Positives (+)	0					
Sum of Negatives (-)	0					
Overall Total	0	0	0	0	0	
Weighted Total	0	0	0	0	0	

Pugh Matrix — Project Name / Project Manager / Date — VALUE GENERATION PARTNERS

Regardless of your Pugh matrix template, format, and layout, it is a useful tool and approach to consider when determining the best possible design option among several alternative concepts.

Wishing you much success in your pursuit of selecting the best design option, thereby generating greater value in your organization!

RACI

RACI is a role-assignment matrix that helps to clarify and define the roles and assignments for large complex projects, cross-functional processes, and cross-departmental initiatives. It is a powerful tool used to depict roles – **R**esponsible, **A**ccountable, **C**onsulted, or **In**formed – for each activity.

Section 5: Tool Selection and Use

The role – such as project manager, sponsor, etc., rather than the person – is listed on the RACI matrix and then correlated to the assignment type, as follows:

- **R**esponsible is the role assigned to complete the activity
- **A**ccountable is the role with approval authority to make decisions and delegate responsibility of the activity; the role identified as accountable is also responsible for the completion of the activity, if no other role is assigned as **R**esponsible in the RACI matrix; this is the only case when a role may be assigned to more than one assignment type
- **C**onsulted is the role that is typically assigned to a subject matter expert (SME) who provides input, advice, and two-way communication regarding the activities
- **I**nformed is the role that is kept updated through one-way communication on progress and completion of activities

There are variations of the RACI matrix that you may find; they include:

- RACIO – Responsible, Accountable, Consulted, Informed, Omitted
- RACI-VS – Responsible, Accountable, Consulted, Informed, Verifier, Signatory
- RAEW – Responsible, Authority, Expertise, Work
- RASCI – Responsible, Accountable, Support, Consulted, Informed
- RASI – Responsible, Accountable, Support, Informed
- RATSI – Responsible, Authority, Task, Support, Informed

A RACI matrix may be used when:

- Activities span several departments or functions
- Project is large and complex, with many roles and activities
- Effort or work is cross-functional in nature
- Work is performed across several businesses, customers, or suppliers

Benefits of a RACI matrix include:

- Provide clarification on roles and assignment types

Section 5: Tool Selection and Use

- Provide a consistent approach for role assignment
- Provide a collaborative team environment
- Provide an approach for efficiently and effectively communicating role assignments

RACI Matrix Process:

1. Assemble a team of stakeholders who are vested in the role assignment initiative
2. List roles across the top axis of the RACI matrix
3. Add activities along the side axis of the RACI matrix
4. Correlate roles and activities by adding an assignment type (i.e.: **R**esponsible, **A**ccountable, **C**onsulted, or **I**nformed)
5. Communicate RACI matrix role assignments, as appropriate and necessary

RACI Matrix Process

- Assemble team
- Add the roles
- Add the activities
- Add the assignment type
- Communicate

While your RACI matrix template may vary slightly, it will likely contain many of the components found in the following example. This image depicts a basic RACI matrix template, along with its elements.

VALUE GENERATION PARTNERS — RACI Matrix

Project Name:					
Project Manager:					
Date:					
Responsible - Accountable - Consulted - Informed					
	Role	Role	Role	Role	Role
Activity					
Activity					
Activity					
Activity					
Activity					
Activity					
Activity					

Section 5: Tool Selection and Use

RACI matrix is a powerful tool for identifying and communicating role assignments.

Wishing you much success in your pursuit of role assignment and activity completion, thereby generating greater value in your organization!

Seven Basic Quality Tools

An essential set of graphical, visual tools for your operational excellence toolbox is the seven basic quality tools. Spawned from teachings of W. Edwards Deming and Kaoru Ishikawa sometime around 1950, these tools have become mainstays in a quality professional's toolbox. Included in PMI®'s PMBOK® 5th Edition, the tools are widely used in all types of projects. The seven basic quality tools may be used independently or in combination with other approaches and methodologies and as elements of problem solving, development, transformation, or continuous improvement initiatives.

Seven basic quality tools:

1. **Cause-and-Effect Diagram** – visual tool, depicted in the following image, used to identify potential causes of an effect, such as a defect or problem for further root-cause analysis

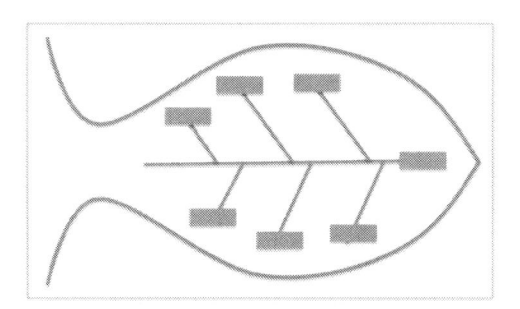

2. **Check Sheet** – template-style tool, depicted in the following image, used to collect, tally, total, and analyze data for further action

Section 5: Tool Selection and Use

Check Sheet								
Project Name:								
Project Manager:						Date:		
Defect/Issue	Sun	Mon	Tues	Wed	Thurs	Fri	Sat	Total
								0
								0
								0
								0
								0
								0
								0
Total	0	0	0	0	0	0	0	0

3. **Control Charts** – graphical tools used to understand and analyze process changes and variation, over time, as depicted in the following images

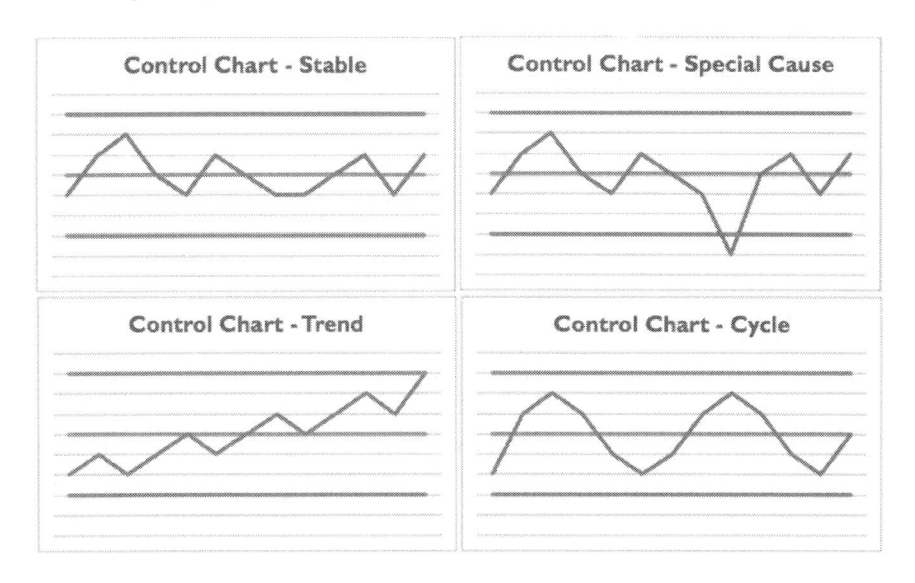

Control Chart - Stable

Control Chart - Special Cause

Control Chart - Trend

Control Chart - Cycle

4. **Histogram** – graphical tool, depicted in the following images, used to display and analyze the shape of a frequency distribution of occurrences for a variable data set

Section 5: Tool Selection and Use

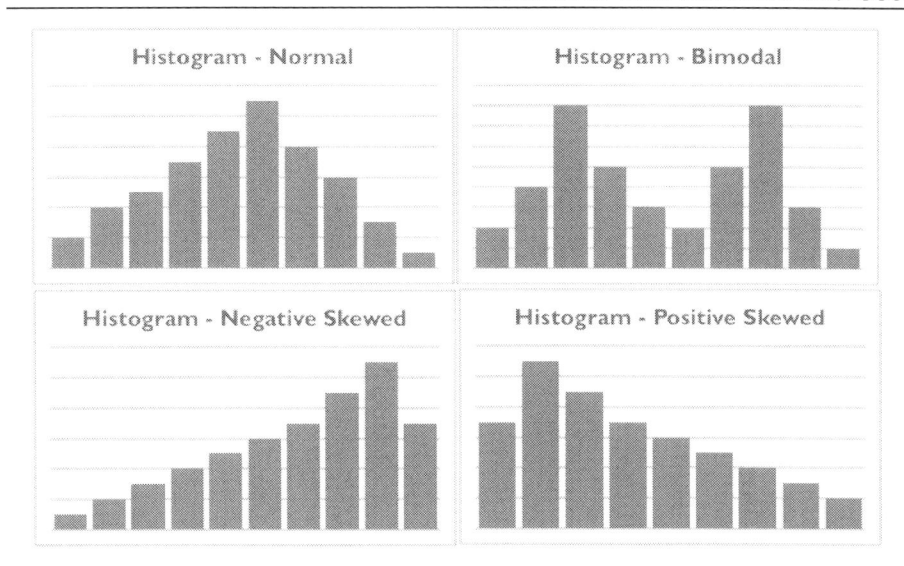

5. **Pareto Chart** – graphical tool, depicted in the following image, used to identify significant categories on which to focus additional or continued efforts

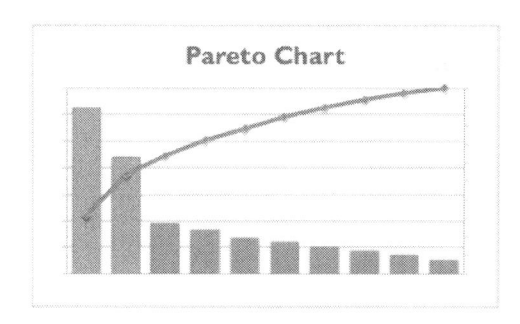

6. **Scatter Diagram** – graphical tool used to compare and analyze two sets of input variable data for a correlation or relationship, as depicted in the following images

Section 5: Tool Selection and Use

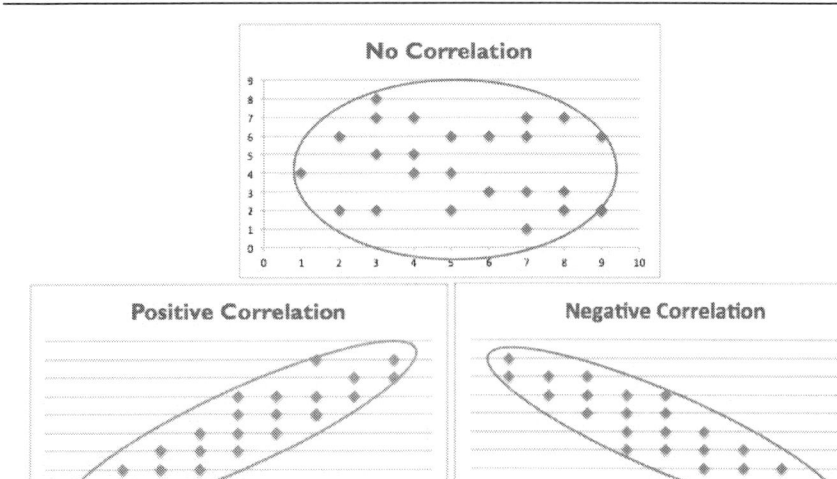

7. **Stratification** – graphical tool, depicted in the following image, used to analyze separations or patterns in a data set, based on two or more input variables

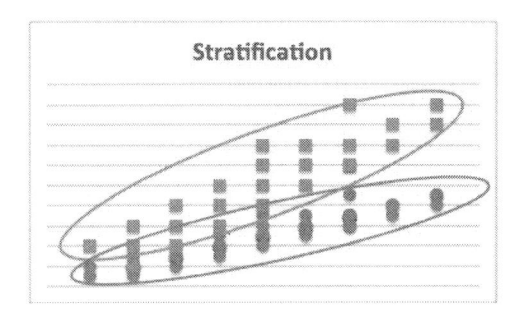

Wishing you much success in your pursuit of selecting appropriate quality tools, thereby generating greater value in your organization!

SIPOC

When you hear the term SIPOC, you might think the discussion is related to a Saturday morning cartoon or an alien monster! However, a **SIPOC** is a document summarizing a project's high-level process, including **S**uppliers, **I**nputs, **P**rocess, **O**utputs and **C**ustomers. It is an

Section 5: Tool Selection and Use

essential tool for any operational excellence, continuous improvement, or transformation project. A completed SIPOC includes a list of the suppliers to the process, inputs to the process, the process itself, outputs of the process, and a list of customers of the process. Included in my SIPOC template is an additional column, titled "CTC," or Critical-To-Customer; it contains a list of the critical-to-customer characteristics expected *from* the process *by* the customer *of* the process.

A SIPOC may be useful when:

- A process is being analyzed as part of a transformation or improvement project
- Team members are not familiar with the process and its elements
- Process documentation is outdated or it is necessary to define a new process
- Procedures, work instructions, and/or training materials are being developed

Benefits of a SIPOC include:

- Provide input for training materials and process documentation
- Provide a starting point for process improvement or transformation
- Provide a consistent approach for analyzing and improving a process
- Provide a simple and high-level view of the process and its elements
- Provide a collaborative team environment

SIPOC Documentation Process:

1. Assemble a cross-functional team of subject matter experts (SMEs)
2. Draw the SIPOC diagram or project the electronic template on a screen
3. Define the high-level process (beginning to end) in a few steps as a vertical block diagram in the process section of the SIPOC
    a. The order in which the columns of the SIPOC template are completed may vary depending on the team and the facilitator

Section 5: Tool Selection and Use

      b. This flow below is detailed as I usually facilitate groups and complete the template
4. Document the outputs from the process including materials, services, and information
5. Document the internal and external customers that receive the outputs of the process (customers may also be suppliers)
6. Document the inputs to the process including materials, services, and information
7. Document the internal and external suppliers of the inputs to the process (suppliers may also be customers)
8. Added to the traditional SIPOC, you may wish to document the critical-to-customer (CTC) characteristics expected from the process; the CTCs must be verified with customers of the process

SIPOC Documentation Process

Assemble the team → Document the customers
↓
Create the SIPOC diagram → Document the inputs
↓
Define the process → Document the suppliers
↓
Document the outputs → Document CTCs

A SIPOC may be used as an input to documenting and improving processes. While your SIPOC template may vary slightly, it will likely contain many of the components found in the following example. This image depicts a basic SIPOC template, along with its elements.

VALUE GENERATION PARTNERS — SIPOC

Project Name:				Project Manager:		Date:
Suppliers	Inputs	Process	Outputs	Customers		CTCs

SIPOC is a powerful tool for identifying and documenting the complete list of process elements.

Wishing you much success in your pursuit of documenting process elements, thereby generating greater value in your organization!

Section 5: Tool Selection and Use

Six Thinking Hats

As a leader, manager, or facilitator, leading teams and individuals in the thinking process is key to success in every organization's culture. Edward de Bono is the author of Six Thinking Hats, a book that defines an approach for teams to conduct parallel thinking, thereby promoting focus, creativity, and productive participation. It is based on six metaphorical hats of specific color and purpose, which may be worn – metaphorically – to direct thoughts, using a process, in order to achieve a desired outcome.

By leading a team through the process of wearing and switching between six hats, the team becomes much more cohesive and productive than if left to random-thinking processes. Parallel thinking indicates that all participants "wear" the same color hat at the same time.

Thinking approach and focus by hat color:

- **Black** – considers decisions and reasoning with careful understanding of risks
- **Blue** – focuses on ensuring the thinking process is followed through action and structure
- **Green** – uses creativity and innovation to generate new ideas and alternatives
- **Red** – emotional and intuitive approach of ideation based on instinct
- **White** – emphasizes factual understanding through data and information
- **Yellow** – optimistic approach to finding value and benefits from

Section 5: Tool Selection and Use

an outcome

Benefits of Six Thinking Hats include:

- Generate innovative ideas and solutions
- Provide a collaborative team environment
- Determine value while mitigating risks
- Increase focus on goals and outcomes
- Provide structure for team dynamics and thinking
- Provide a consistent approach for generating and evaluating ideas
- Provide an approach for effectively thinking as a team

Below is an example of using Six Thinking Hats to make a decision to lease, buy, or build.

A team is facilitated using Six Thinking Hats to make a decision (lease, buy, or build) for expansion of a warehouse facility. The facilitator, being well versed on the Six Thinking Hats technique, uses the blue *process* hat to manage the session, setting the tone and direction. If the thought process drifts from intended topic and style, the facilitator applies blue hat thinking to pull back and redirect the team.

The facilitator proceeds with green *creative* hat thinking to brainstorm various alternatives associated with any of the three choices (lease, buy, or build). Brainstorming elements include warehouse location alternatives, square footage needed, types of storage and shelving, docking needs, etc. There are moments of red *emotional* hat thinking by some participants; they become passionate about the aesthetics of the building when considering an older, leased building versus a new building. While these are important considerations, the facilitator pauses the discussions for a blue hat moment to refocus, and includes aesthetics into the brainstorming considerations.

The team switches to white *fact* hat thinking, reviewing and analyzing data and information relevant to the decision. The team reviews short-term and long-term costs of leasing, buying, or building. Members determine when each option would be available to occupy and consider the implications of such on their customers' needs. Revenue, gross margins, net profits, and cash flows are calculated based

Section 5: Tool Selection and Use

on move-in dates of each option. Impacts to the workforce are evaluated and discussed.

The facilitator switches to yellow *optimism* hat thinking to define the potential value and benefits resulting from green hat brainstorming and white hat data analysis. Then, using black *risk* hat thinking, the team determines potential pitfalls and mitigations from selecting any of the alternatives.

By using a Six Thinking Hat approach, the team considers three alternatives in a structured, factual, emotional, risk, creative, and beneficial perspective. The team conducts a presentation of the process and results to leadership, gaining full support for the decision to buy an existing building for their warehouse needs.

While facilitating a team or group, it may be helpful to consider these tools, as listed below, to assist when using specific hat colors:

- **Black** – fault tree analysis, risk management plan, FMEA, control plan
- **Blue** – agenda, action plan, SMART goals, ground rules
- **Green** – brainstorming, nominal group technique, Pugh matrix, House of Quality
- **Red** – force field analysis, mind mapping, pairwise comparison, brainstorming, nominal group technique
- **White** – seven basic quality tools, data collection plan, data analysis tools, graphical analysis tools
- **Yellow** – impact/effort matrix, decision tree, cause-and-effect diagram

Six Thinking Hats is a powerful approach that may be used as a facilitation technique during continuous improvement events or throughout the phases of A3 Thinking, Lean Six Sigma, or Design for Lean Six Sigma. It may be applied to many of the tools employed for elements of an operational excellence, transformation, or continuous improvement initiative.

Wishing you much success in your pursuit of focused, creative, and productive thinking, thereby generating greater value in your organization!

Section 5: Tool Selection and Use

Solution-Selection Matrix

A solution-selection matrix is a powerful selection tool used to choose between multiple solution alternatives during a problem-solving or continuous improvement project. A solution-selection matrix may also be used as an alternative to a Pugh matrix for choosing the best design concept for a new process, product, or service.

A solution-selection matrix may be used when:

- The current process has problems, issues, errors, or defects
- The current process, product, or service requires improvement
- Choosing the best solution among several potential solutions
- The current solution is not meeting customer requirements or performing as required

Benefits of a solution-selection matrix include:

- Reduce emotion and bias from the decision-making process
- Provide a consistent approach for selecting the best solution among several options
- Save cost and time by efficiently and effectively selecting the best solution
- Provide a collaborative team environment

Solution-Selection Matrix Process:

1. Assemble a cross-functional team of subject matter experts who will be prepared for the solution-selection session with pre-work on the topic
2. Draw a solution-selection matrix on a board or flipchart, or project an electronic matrix on a screen
3. List or brainstorm potential solutions to eliminate the current problems or issues
4. List or brainstorm selection criteria to evaluate potential solutions; the selection criteria may be determined with input from the project sponsor

Solution-Selection Process

Assemble the team → List potential solutions → List and weight selection criteria → Rank solutions (1, 5, 9) → Determine solution scores → Select best solutions

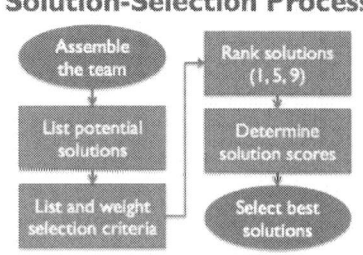

200

Section 5: Tool Selection and Use

5. Determine a weight factor for each of the selection criteria; weights may be determined using pairwise comparison or simply ranking on a scale of 1 to 5
6. Evaluate each potential solution against the criteria, and enter a rank of 1 if the solution "does not meet" the criteria, 5 for "somewhat meets" the criteria, or 9 for "fully meets" the criteria
7. Determine the weighted score by multiplying each selection criteria weight by the individual solution score, then summing the total for each concept; note that the matrix template performs these calculations
8. Determine which solution(s) to implement in order to eliminate issues and problems with the current solution or process

An example using a solution-selection matrix is a continuous improvement team analyzing several potential solutions to reduce defects found during testing at a software development company. The team analyzes the process and the causes of the defects, and then develops a list of eight potential solutions to prevent the defects. The potential solutions are evaluated against the selection criteria listed in the matrix; those potential solutions with the highest scores are selected for implementation.

While your solution-selection matrix template may vary slightly, it will likely contain many of the components found in the following example. This image depicts a basic solution-selection matrix template, along with its elements.

Section 5: Tool Selection and Use

Solution-Selection Matrix

Project Name:										
Project Manager:						Date:				
			Selection Criteria							
			Low Effort	High Impact	Acceptable Cost	Acceptable Time	Acceptable Risk	Resources Available	Cultural Acceptance	Addresses Root Cause
			Weight								Total Score	Implement (Y or N)
Output (y) or CTC	Root Cause (x)	Potential Solution	(1=No, 5=Somewhat, 9=Yes)									
											0	
											0	
											0	
											0	
											0	
											0	
											0	

Regardless of your solution-selection matrix template, format, and layout, it is a useful tool and approach to consider when determining the best possible solution among several alternative solutions.

Wishing you much success in your pursuit of selecting the best solution, thereby generating greater value in your organization!

Status Report

Status reporting and feedback are fundamental to the successful execution and governance of a project lifecycle. Status reports are conducted on a weekly, bi-weekly, or monthly cycle, depending on the size, complexity, duration of the project, and depending on stakeholder needs. While a status report contributes to the success of project execution, it is very useful for other endeavors in business and may be considered for any undertaking or initiative.

A status report is used when:

- The project impacts external customers
- The project is important to the organization's strategies and suc-

Section 5: Tool Selection and Use

cess
- An active project begins the planning and execution phase of the lifecycle
- Sponsor, stakeholders, and senior leaders are heavily engaged and interested in the project

Benefits of a status report include:

- Provide an informative and collaborative team environment
- Save cost and time through accountability, visibility, and feedback loop
- Provide a consistent, efficient, and effective approach for reporting project status, health, accomplishments, issues, and risks
- Increase focus and attention on project governance and accountability by key stakeholders and project team

Status Reporting Cycle:

1. Prepare and update the status report with current project information
   a. Brief overview of the project
   b. Activities and actions planned for the next reporting cycle
   c. Accomplishments since the last reporting cycle
   d. Metrics for measuring the project health and success
   e. Issues and risks, along with plans for resolution
2. Schedule and conduct status report update with project sponsor, team, and key stakeholders
3. Gather feedback on project status and health
4. Incorporate feedback into project plan and schedule

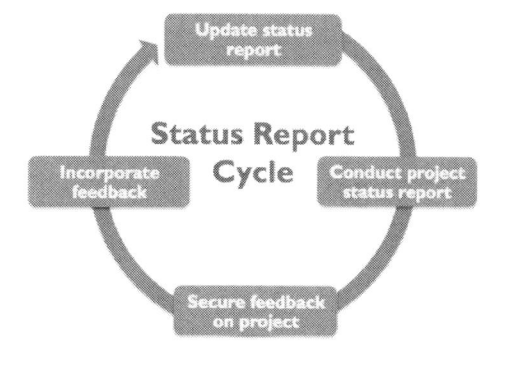

While your status report template may vary slightly, it will likely contain many of the components found in the following example. This image depicts a basic status report template, along with its elements.

Section 5: Tool Selection and Use

Project Status Report

Project Name:				
Project Overview			**Metrics**	**Status**
Date:				
Project Manager:				
Project Sponsor:				
Deliverables:				
Goal:			**Accomplishments**	
Scope:				
Metrics:				
Other:				
Project Next Steps	**Due**	**Status**		
			Issues/Risks and Resolutions	**Status**

Regardless of your status report template, format, and layout, it is fundamental for larger and more complex projects to include a status report as part of the lifecycle review process.

Wishing you much success in your pursuit of status updates, thereby generating greater value in your organization!

SWOT Analysis

SWOT Analysis ... what a great tool to determine the **S**trengths, **W**eaknesses, **O**pportunities, and **T**hreats of a business, strategy, service, product, project, department, or a function! SWOT is often credited to Albert Humphrey of Stanford University, when, in the 1960s and 1970s, he led research projects using data from many top companies.

As you can see, a SWOT analysis can be performed as a transformational effort, a strategic planning tool, or a precursor to cultural change for every type of entity or topic. It can be beneficial when performed as a proactive event to determine directional corrections prior

Section 5: Tool Selection and Use

to a change implementation or as a reactive session to determine changes to improve an existing situation.

A SWOT analysis identifies internal characteristics and external elements that are significant to influencing or achieving a desired outcome of the SWOT topic. The SWOT analysis matrix is divided into two categories (Internal and External) and four elements (Strengths, Weaknesses, Opportunities, and Threats).

- **Internal** categories are *strengths* and *weaknesses*
    - **Strengths** are internal characteristics that will drive achievement of the desired outcome
    - **Weaknesses** are internal characteristics that may prevent the desired outcome, if not reinforced
- **External** elements are *opportunities* and *threats*
    - **Opportunities** are external elements that can be leveraged to achieve the desired outcome
    - **Threats** are external elements that may prevent achieving the desired outcome, if not mitigated

A SWOT analysis may be used as:

- Input to transformational or operational excellence programs
- Input to a project plan
- A determination of initiative, program, or project viability
- A precursor to strategic planning
- A team approach tool for defining input to programs and projects

Benefits of SWOT analysis include:

- Provide valuable input for strategic planning initiatives, programs, and projects
- Proactive approach to determine which initiatives, programs, and projects to undertake
- Provide input for developing a project plan and assigning resources
- Provide a collaborative team environment
- Bring together diverse backgrounds and experiences

Section 5: Tool Selection and Use

Follow the steps below for a simple approach to conduct a SWOT analysis:

1. Assemble a cross-functional team of subject matter experts (SMEs), who will be prepared for the session upon completing pre-work on the SWOT analysis topic
2. Describe and document the reason, objective, and intended outcome for performing an analysis on the SWOT topic
3. Conduct the SWOT analysis by brainstorming a list of internal characteristics and external elements related to the situation or desired outcome
4. Prioritize the list – by category and element – for actions to leverage, mitigate, overcome, or exploit
    a. Map the strengths to opportunities, which can be leveraged, and to threats, which can be mitigated
    b. Understand weaknesses that need to be overcome to take advantage of opportunities, and that might be exploited by threats
5. Develop an action plan describing "who, what, and when," based on the prioritization you did in the previous step
6. Define a follow-up plan, which includes a schedule, to ensure actions are completed as planned
7. Re-run the SWOT analysis, as part of a continuous improvement cycle, based on changes in the internal or external environment

SWOT Analysis Process

Assemble team → State the SWOT topic → Brainstorm SWOT characteristics and elements → Prioritize characteristics and elements → Develop an action plan → Follow-up on actions → Rerun SWOT

An example of using SWOT analysis is a cross-functional team at a medium-sized retail clothing chain, working on its clothing lines and floor layouts for the new shopping season. The team uses the SWOT analysis to understand its internal strengths and weaknesses with its current offerings and store layouts, as well as its external opportunities and threats based on consumer buying trends, competitor offerings, and competitor store designs. Using the SWOT information, the team designs new store layouts and defines a plan for clothing lines to offer during the upcoming season.

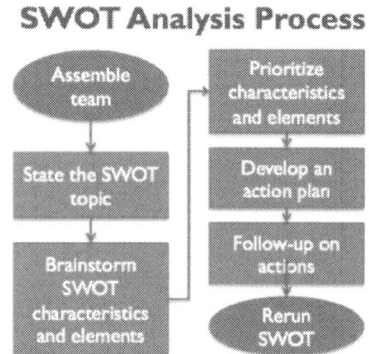

Section 5: Tool Selection and Use

A simple matrix tool, as noted in the following image, will be helpful for facilitating a SWOT analysis session.

VALUE GENERATIONPARTNERS **SWOT Analysis**				
Facilitator:		Date:	
SWOT Topic:			
Internal Strengths	**Score**	**Internal Weaknesses**	**Score**
External Opportunities	**Score**	**External Threats**	**Score**

Wishing you much success in your pursuit of strengthening your results and outcomes through conducting SWOT analyses, thereby generating greater value in your organization!

Training Plan

Most projects result in a new process, product, or service, which require some amount and level of training. A well-executed training plan is an important artifact to include in the project toolbox to ensure successful execution of planned project results. While a training plan is critical to the success of launching a new process, product, or service, it is very useful for other endeavors in business and may be considered in other undertakings, as well.

In today's global and fast-paced environment, it is difficult to find time to conduct training sessions, so the necessary training may be delivered in the several methods:

Section 5: Tool Selection and Use

- **eLearning** – participants take the training via computer at their own pace and time
- **Instructor-led** – participants attend an in-class session that is facilitated by an instructor
- **Virtual** – participants dial-in and logon to a web-based training session that is led by a remote instructor
- **Blended learning** – participants may take the training in a combination of instructor-led, virtual, and/or eLearning sessions

A training plan is useful when:

- A project results in a new process, product, or service
- A project crosses many functions or departments
- The project impacts safety, quality, or customer service

Benefits of developing a training plan include:

- Provide a consistent approach for analyzing, developing, delivering, and validating training
- Provide an approach for efficiently and effectively executing training
- Provide a collaborative team environment
- Save cost and time by developing and delivering training appropriate to the project

Training Plan Process:

1. Training topic is identified as part of the project deliverables
2. A training needs analysis and materials design/development owner is identified and assigned
3. Trainer is identified and assigned
4. Training logistics – including participants, delivery date, training duration, and delivery method – are determined and defined
5. Training is delivered, evaluated, and adjusted
6. Training results are validated to ensure the training intent was achieved

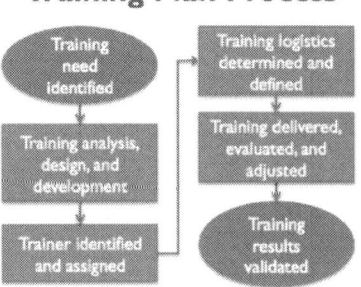

Training Plan Process

Training need identified → Training logistics determined and defined ↓
Training analysis, design, and development → Training delivered, evaluated, and adjusted ↓
Trainer identified and assigned → Training results validated

Section 5: Tool Selection and Use

While your training plan template may vary slightly, it will likely contain many of the components found in the following example. This image depicts a basic training plan template, along with its elements.

\multicolumn{4}{c	}{**Training Plan**}					
\multicolumn{4}{l	}{Project Name:}	\multicolumn{5}{l	}{Project Manager:}
\multicolumn{4}{c	}{Analyze - Design - Develop}	\multicolumn{5}{c	}{Deliver - Evaluate - Adjust - Validate}
Who	What	When	Other	Who	When	How		Other
Owner	Topic	Due Date	Status Comments	Trainer	Participant(s)	Date	Duration	Method	Results Comments

Regardless of your training plan template, format, and layout, it may be necessary to include such a plan in the project toolbox and to review it during project review meetings.

Wishing you much success in your pursuit of knowledge transfer, thereby generating greater value in your organization!

Summary

Successfully achieving operational excellence is the culmination of bringing together these key elements, all of which are consistently and repeatedly approached with commitment, passion, rigor, and discipline.

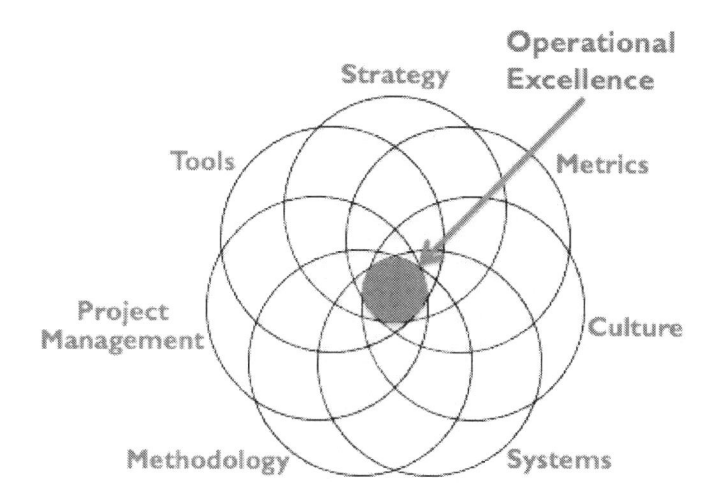

- **Strategy** – leadership creates vision and values for the organization; these are distilled into strategic focus and direction
- **Metrics** – scorecards balanced to strategies, and cascading through entire organization
- **Culture** – all individuals understand the strategy, and are authorized for, accountable for, and owners of achieving the strategic vision through continuous improvement of processes, products, and services
- **Systems** – organization implements holistic, integrated quality management system and processes
- **Methodology** – applying rigor and discipline of Design for Lean Six Sigma, Lean Six Sigma, A3 Thinking, or Theory of Constraints
- **Project Management** – applying rigor and discipline of Project Management Institute's (PMI®'s) Project Management Body of Knowledge (PMBOK®)
- **Tools** – solution delivery (processes, products, and services), problem solving, and continuous improvement

Summary

Employing these critical elements listed above – along with a foundation of well-communicated and understood purpose, vision, mission, and set of values – creates operational excellence.

We wish you much success in your pursuit of operational excellence, thereby generating greater value in your organization!

Index

5

5 Why
   Root-Cause Analysis, 41, 47, 64, 123, 124, 125, 135, 151

A

A3 Thinking, 54, 55
   Lean Thinking, 2, 14, 39, 51, 52, 54, 55, 64, 124, 199, 211
Action Plan, 3, 6, 34, 42, 45, 47, 68, 80, 82, 88, 89, 91, 117, 121, 126, 127, 128, 134, 148, 151, 153, 154, 172, 175, 177, 199, 206
Adjourning, 37
Affinity Diagram, 41, 64, 128, 129, 130, 134
Agenda, 130, 131, 199
Alderfer's ERG Theory, 30
Analyze, 53, 56, 58, 60, 68, 148, 151
Archimedes' Principle, 103
Artifact, 69, 71, 75, 83, 88, 93, 98, 103, 106, 108, 111, 113, 115, 117, 207

B

Balanced Scorecard, 3, 9, 12, 14
Belonging, 32
Bill Gates, 115
Blended learning, 208
Block Diagrams, 181, 182, 195
Brainstorming, ix, 41, 47, 64, 116, 125, 128, 132, 133, 134, 135, 136, 137, 166, 171, 174, 175, 176, 177, 198, 199, 206
Budget, 11, 51, 66, 67, 68, 70, 79, 82, 99, 104, 109, 111, 112, 114
Business Case Proposal, 69, 72, 73, 74

C

C&E
   Cause-and-Effect Diagram, Fishbone Diagram, Ishikawa Diagram, 41, 64, 129, 134, 135, 137, 142, 145, 151, 185, 199
Cascading Scorecards, 7, 12, 14
Cause-and-Effect Matrix, 136
   X-Y Matrix, 41, 136, 137, 138, 185
Celebrate, 68, 82
Change Control Plan, 99, 104, 106, 109, 113, 114, 115, 117, 127, 131
Change Leaders, 19, 21
Change Leadership, 19, 22
Change Log, 70
Change Resistors, 21
Charter, 65, 69, 75, 158
Checklist, 68, 70, 117, 118, 119, 121, 159
Close-out/Hand-off Plan, 70
Cognitive Evaluation Theory (CET) of Motivation, 29
Communication Plan, 65, 70, 98, 99
Concise, 33, 35, 54, 65, 102, 103
Contact List, 65, 70, 93, 94
Continuous Improvement, i, iii, ix, xi, 1, 2, 19, 39, 40, 42, 45, 47, 48, 51, 52, 54, 58, 60, 64, 76, 103, 116, 117, 131, 139, 141, 157, 191, 195, 199, 200, 201, 206, 211
Control, 53, 56, 65, 70, 82, 86, 96, 100, 105, 107, 109, 113, 114, 123, 138, 139, 140, 154, 185, 192
Control Plan, 65, 70, 113, 114, 123, 138, 140

213

Index

CoQ
  Cost of Quality, 49
Core Requirements, 168, 170
Correlation, 11, 161, 163, 193
Cost of quality, 49
CTC, 42
  Critical-to-Customer, 8, 42, 43, 137, 195, 196
CTQ
  Critical-to-Quality, 137

D

Data Collection Plan, 71, 123, 141, 145
Define, 5, 6, 8, 26, 27, 42, 45, 52, 53, 56, 60, 73, 79, 87, 95, 96, 127, 129, 147, 151, 153, 184, 195, 206
Delighters, 170
Deming Cycle, 54
Deployment Flowchart
  Swimlane Map, 181, 184
Design for Lean Six Sigma (DfLSS), 2, 39, 51, 53, 59, 60, 62, 64, 199, 211
Desired, 16, 19, 131, 139, 162, 168, 170, 172, 197, 205, 206
Detection, 156, 157
DfLSS
  Design for Lean Six Sigma, 39, 51, 53, 54, 59, 62
DFMEA
  Design FMEA, 155
DFX
  Design for X, 53
Dissatisfiers, 169
DMADV, 51, 53, 54
  IDOV, IDDOV, DMADOV, and DFX, 39, 51, 53, 54, 59, 60, 62
DMAIC, 14, 39, 51, 52, 54, 56, 58, 59, 67, 124
DOWNTIME
  8 Forms of Waste, 46

E

eLearning, 208
ERP
  Enterprise Resource Planning, 153
Esteem, 32
Exciters, 168, 170
Existence, 30
Expected, 14, 35, 43, 47, 73, 81, 91, 146, 147, 148, 150, 168, 169, 195, 196
Experimental, 142
Extrinsic Motivators, 30

F

Facilitation, 28, 40, 133, 154, 177, 199, 207
Fault Tree Analysis (FTA), 148, 149, 151, 199
Financials, 69, 80
Fishbone Diagram, 134
Flowcharts, 181
Flow-down, 9
FMEA
  Failure Modes and Effects Analysis, 41, 71, 123, 140, 142, 145, 151, 154, 155, 156, 157, 199
Force Field Analysis, 71, 123, 152
Forming, 35
FTA
  Fault Tree Analysis, 148

G

Gantt Chart, 65, 94, 97
Governance, 69, 118, 130, 202, 203
Growth, 7, 12, 30

H

Herzberg's Two-Factor Theory, 30, 31
Historical, 142

214

Index

HOQ
　House of Quality, 160
House of Quality (HOQ), 160, 161, 162
Hygiene factors, 31

I

IDOV, 53, 59
Impact/Effort Analysis, 165, 166
Impact/Effort Matrix, 71, 123, 165, 166, 167
Improve, 53, 56, 149, 158
Indifferent, 170
Inform, 85
Informative, 65, 101
Input/Output Process Map, 181, 182
Instructor-led, 208
Intellectual-Asset Repository, 117, 120
Interval, 143
Intrinsic Motivators, 29
Ishikawa Diagram, 134
ISO 9000 Quality Management System, 14, 15, 16
ISO 9001, 14, 15
Issue Log, 70
Issue Management Plan, 99, 104, 106, 109, 111, 112, 117, 127, 131, 140

K

Kano Model, 168
Kano Model Analysis, 123, 163, 168, 169, 170, 171
Kaoru Ishikawa, 134, 191
Key Stakeholders, 84
KPI
　Key Performance Indicator, 12, 13

L

Lean Six Sigma

LSS, 2, 14, 34, 39, 51, 52, 53, 56, 58, 59, 60, 62, 64, 67, 76, 124, 199, 211
Lessons-Learned, 68, 86, 115, 116, 117, 127, 131
Lessons-Learned Plan, 68, 70, 86, 115, 116, 117, 127, 131, 145
Lifecycle, 51, 66, 68, 69, 70, 71, 75, 76, 77, 78, 83, 84, 86, 87, 90, 91, 94, 95, 98, 100, 103, 106, 108, 109, 111, 113, 115, 116, 117, 118, 119, 120, 126, 127, 130, 131, 139, 141, 142, 144, 153, 202, 203, 204
LSS
　Lean Six Sigma, 39, 51, 52, 54, 56

M

MacGyver, 51
Manage, 45, 85, 86, 87, 92, 100
Maslow's Hierarchy of Needs, 30, 31, 32
McClelland's Acquired Needs Theory, 30, 32
Measure, 52, 53, 56, 60
Mind Mapping, 41, 171, 172, 173, 199
Minutes, 73, 75, 101, 102, 103, 130, 131, 133, 177
Mission, 2, 8, 9, 34, 38, 212
Mitigate, 87, 108, 109, 125, 143, 151, 152, 153, 155, 206
Monitor, 20, 23, 33, 47, 85, 127
Motivating Individuals, 32, 33
Motivators, 31
Murphy's Law, 154
Must Haves, 168, 169
Must-Have, 79

N

NASA, 154
　National Aeronautics and Space Administration, 154

215

Index

NGT
  Nominal Group Technique, 123, 176
Nice-to-Have, 79
Nominal, 28, 123, 143, 176, 177
Nominal Group Technique (NGT), 64, 176, 199
Norming, 36
NPD
  New Product Development, 59
NVA
  Non-Value Added, 180
NVAN
  Non-Value Added but Necessary, 180

O

Observational, 142
Occurrence, 113, 156, 157
Operational Excellence, xi, 1, 2, 3, 11, 14, 19, 33, 39, 54, 65, 76, 102, 123, 139, 141, 152, 158, 191, 195, 199, 205, 211, 212
Ordinal, 143

P

Pairwise Comparison, 26, 28, 177, 178, 179
Pareto, 64, 193
PDCA, 54, 55
  PDSA, 14, 39, 51, 52, 54, 55
Performing, 36
Peter Drucker, 12, 19, 158
PFMEA
  Process FMEA, 155
Physiological, 32
PMBOK®
  Project Management Body of Knowledge, 2, 66, 76, 79, 82, 86, 89, 92, 96, 100, 104, 107, 109, 114, 121, 191, 211
PMI®
  Project Management Institute, 2, 66, 67, 76, 79, 82, 86, 89, 92, 96, 100, 104, 107, 109, 114, 121, 191, 211
Primary Stakeholders, 84
Process, xi, 5, 7, 9, 13, 17, 18, 20, 21, 23, 24, 26, 27, 28, 35, 36, 39, 40, 41, 42, 43, 44, 45, 46, 47, 48, 52, 53, 56, 59, 60, 62, 63, 64, 66, 67, 68, 70, 72, 75, 78, 79, 81, 84, 85, 86, 87, 88, 91, 99, 101, 104, 108, 109, 111, 112, 113, 116, 119, 120, 121, 124, 127, 134, 135, 136, 137, 138, 139, 140, 141, 142, 144, 150, 152, 154, 155, 156, 157, 159, 160, 165, 166, 172, 175, 176, 178, 179, 180, 181, 182, 183, 184, 185, 186, 187, 192, 194, 195, 196, 197, 198, 199, 200, 201, 204, 207, 208
Procurement, 70, 104, 106, 107, 108, 131
Project Lifecycle, 51, 66, 68, 69, 70, 71, 75, 76, 77, 78, 83, 84, 86, 87, 90, 91, 94, 95, 98, 100, 103, 106, 108, 109, 111, 113, 115, 116, 117, 118, 119, 120, 126, 127, 130, 131, 139, 141, 142, 144, 153, 202, 203, 204
Project-Close, 68, 119, 120, 121, 122
Pugh
  Concept Selection, 28, 41, 123, 134, 146, 185, 186, 187, 188, 199, 200
Pugh Matrix, 28, 41, 134, 146, 185, 186, 187, 188, 199, 200
Purpose, 2, 8, 9, 16, 34, 37, 38, 40, 45, 48, 197, 212
Pythagorean Theorem, 103

Q

QFD

Index

Quality Function Deployment, 160
QMS
   Quality Management System, 14, 15
Quality Function Deployment (QFD), 160
Quality Management, xi, 2, 14, 15, 16, 17, 18, 99, 103, 104, 105, 106, 109, 116, 127, 131, 211

R

RACI, 23, 41, 43, 44, 45, 64, 71, 123, 188, 189, 190, 191
Relatedness, 30
Requirements, 8, 15, 16, 17, 49, 52, 53, 59, 60, 69, 70, 76, 77, 78, 79, 80, 82, 87, 88, 91, 95, 96, 104, 105, 107, 139, 151, 156, 157, 160, 161, 162, 163, 168, 170, 178, 186, 200
Resource Plan, 15, 89, 90, 91, 92, 93, 97, 99, 104, 106, 109, 116, 127, 153
Retrospective, 142
Reverse, 170
Risk Log, 70
Risk Management Plan, 22, 80, 86, 89, 92, 97, 99, 104, 106, 108, 109, 110, 111, 112, 115, 117, 127, 131, 145, 199
RPN
   Risk Priority Number, 157

S

Safety, 32
Satisfiers, 170
Satisfy, 85
Schedule, xi, 22, 34, 44, 51, 65, 66, 67, 68, 70, 78, 79, 80, 82, 88, 89, 91, 94, 95, 96, 97, 98, 99, 104, 106, 109, 111, 112, 114, 116, 121, 126, 127, 131, 154, 176, 203, 206
Scope, 11, 22, 34, 41, 51, 66, 67, 68, 69, 70, 73, 75, 76, 79, 88, 89, 96, 99, 104, 109, 111, 112, 114, 120, 158, 159
Scorecards, 1, 3, 6, 8, 12, 13, 14, 64, 211
Secondary Stakeholders, 84
Self-Actualization, 32
Seven Basic Quality Tools, 191, 199
Severity, 156, 157
Shainin, 51
SIPOC, 8, 41, 43, 44, 45, 64, 123, 137, 142, 145, 163, 194, 195, 196
Six Sigma, 2, 14, 34, 39, 51, 52, 53, 56, 58, 59, 60, 62, 64, 67, 76, 124, 199, 211
SMART, 123, 158, 159, 160, 199
SME
   Subject Matter Expert, 44, 153, 155, 166, 195, 206
Solution-Selection Matrix, 41, 71, 123, 134, 200
SOW
   Statement of Work, 78, 88
Staffing Plan, 70, 90
Stakeholder Analysis, 70, 85, 86, 153
Storming, 35
Strategic Goals, 9, 10, 11, 29
Strategy Maps, 3, 6, 7, 8, 9, 13
Stratification, 144
Swimlane, 43, 44
   Deployment Flowchart, 43, 44, 45, 181, 184
SWOT, 8, 23, 41, 123, 204, 205, 206, 207

T

TIM U WOOD
   8 Forms of Waste, 46
Toolbox, xii, 22, 62, 65, 68, 69, 71, 75, 80, 83, 87, 88, 89, 90, 93, 94, 98, 100, 103, 105, 106,

217

Index

108, 110, 111, 112, 113, 115, 117, 119, 122, 128, 139, 141, 146, 191, 207, 209
Training Plan, 22, 42, 99, 106, 109, 117, 127, 207, 208, 209
Transformation, i, iii, xi, 2, 3, 4, 5, 6, 19, 33, 39, 65, 76, 102, 123, 139, 141, 152, 158, 191, 195, 199

U

Unexpected, 111, 168, 170

V

VA
  Value Added, 180
Value Generation Journey, xi, 3, 19, 39, 65, 124
Value Stream, 9, 63

Values, 1, 2, 4, 7, 8, 9, 25, 147, 148, 167, 211, 212
Virtual, 34, 208
Vision, 1, 2, 4, 7, 8, 9, 13, 20, 22, 34, 35, 75, 211, 212
VOC
  Voice of Customer/Competitor, 163, 168

W

Wait-and-Seers, 21
WBS
  Work Breakdown Structure, 70, 87, 88, 89, 90

X

X-Y Matrix
  Cause-and-Effect Matrix, 136, 140, 142

Printed in Great Britain
by Amazon